The Chartered Institute of Management Accountants

CIMA
PUBLISHING

Information System Development in the Small Firm

The Use of Management Accounting

Falconer Mitchell
Professor of Management Accounting
University of Edinburgh

Gavin Reid
Professor of Economics and Director, CRIEFF
University of St Andrews

Julia Smith
Lecturer in Accounting, Cardiff Business School
Cardiff University

This publication arises from the research project 'The nature and development of management accounting in SMEs' which was funded with a research grant from the CIMA Research Foundation. The award of a Research Foundation grant, and the publication of findings in this format, indicates that the recipient has successfully passed two separate peer review processes, which also involved practitioner assessors. The views expressed in this publication are the authors' own, and do not necessarily represent those of CIMA.

Acknowledgements

The authors would like to acknowledge with gratitude the assistance of several parties to this research. First, thanks are due to the Research Foundation of the Chartered Institute of Management Accountants (CIMA) for sponsoring the fieldwork stage of the project. Gratitude must be expressed also to the Leverhulme Trust for funding the earlier study, from which this work developed. Finally, thanks must be given to the enterprise movement in Scotland, including the Enterprise Trusts and the small-business owner-managers, without whom this work could never have been undertaken.

Any errors of omission or commission remain the responsibility of the authors.

First published in 2000 by:
The Chartered Institute of Management Accountants
63 Portland Place
London
W1B 1AB

ISBN 1 85971 453 6

Contents

Abbreviations

ACA	Association of Certified Accountants
AIM	Alternative investment market
AIS	Accounting information system
CIMA	Chartered Institute of Management Accountants
DCF	Discounted cash flow
DDBMS	Distributed database management system
EC	European Community
EDP	Electronic data processing
GDP	Gross domestic product
IFAC	International Federation of Accountants
IS	Information system
IT	Information technology
LISREL	Linear structural relations model
MAS	Management accounting system
MIS	Management information system
PEU	Perceived environmental uncertainty
R&D	Research and development
ROI	Return on investment
SB	Statutory plus budget information
SBA	Statutory plus budget plus additional information
SME	Small and medium-sized enterprises
SPSS	Statistical package for the social sciences
ST	Statutory information
SWOT	Strengths, weaknesses, opportunities and threats
USP	Unique selling point
Y	Performance

Executive Summary

- Sets out three modern theories of how management accounting information enhances performance;
- provides the latest evidence on the link between performance and accounting information system development;
- shows how in practice both struggling and successful small firms use information for improved decision-making and control;
- reports on how small firms cope with the complexity and reliability of information;
- statistically estimates the effects of markets, strategy, production and technology on the best organisation of the small firm;
- shows which factors determine the complexity of management accounting systems;
- presents practical case studies of how information systems can adapt to changed circumstances.

This work is grounded in contemporary evidence on current practice in small firms. Such evidence was gathered by face-to-face interviews within the firms over a four-year period. It covers all aspects of operations and strategy, with particularly detailed attention being given to the development and handling of accounting information.

After setting out the relevant theoretical and empirical background, the work uses this evidence to investigate the link between the form of the firm and the contingencies which impinge upon its information system. It does so using both qualitative and quantitative evidence. Thus concrete case studies of the experience of specific firms are backed up with statistical evidence of general patterns of behaviour across the sample of firms.

The work shows that accounting information can help a small firm in two major ways. First, for the successful, growing firm, in a dynamic and competitive environment, it is used to integrate operational considerations within long-term strategic plans. Second, for the struggling firm, it is used to manage short-term problems in areas such as costing, expenditure and cash flow, by appropriate monitoring and control. Further, it shows how complex factors mould and develop the management accounting system. These include external factors, like competitiveness and internal factors such as the emergence of hierarchy.

Overall, the work suggests that the small firm need not be at the mercy of internal and external forces. In all circumstances, it can take rational steps to modify monitoring and control mechanisms, typically by adjustments to its information system, to the end of enhancing economic performance.

1

The Research Setting

1.1 Introduction

This study is designed to explore the nature of management accounting in the small firm. It is not, however, merely a static or descriptive study of the management accounting techniques and systems prevalent in small firms at a particular point in time. Its aims are more analytical and dynamic than this, as it is primarily concerned with investigating the factors in the organisational and environmental context of the small firm which are instrumental in the emergence and subsequent development (or lack of development) of management accounting. Thus, while the study does contain material on *what* form management accounting takes in small firms, it has a much greater emphasis on *why* management accounting exists in its current form in small firms and *why* and *how* it changes in particular ways over time.

To address these issues, data has been gathered from a sample of Scottish small firms over a five-year period.[1] This information has been analysed against a framework of three, relatively contemporary, economic theories (contingency theory, agency theory and markets and hierarchies) which have recently been applied to provide a fundamental rationale for the management accounting discipline (see Jordan, 1999). Thus, the study has an economic orientation but one in which economic theory is used to help explain and understand observation from the real world, about the nature, role and development of management accounting in small firms.[2]

1.2 The small firm

The small firm[3] is an important component of a modern market economy and indeed could even be considered the major part of the UK business constituency. In the early 1990s, 99 per cent of UK businesses fell into this category, while 58 per cent of

---

1 See Reid (1999) for an account of the sampling frame. Essentially, it was based on a stratified random sample from eighteen geographical areas within lowland Scotland. Ports of entry were the Enterprise Trusts (business incubators). There were 150 new micro-firms in the sample.

2 The account of the study provided in this chapter is a development of the brief treatment in Mitchell et al. (1998).

3 The Companies Act 1985 (Sections 246, 247 and 249) lays down the qualifying conditions for small and medium-sized companies as follows: 'Small' – turnover under £2.8m, balance sheet total not more than £1.4m and average number of employees not exceeding 50; 'medium-sized' – turnover under £11.2m, balance sheet total not more than £5.6m and average number of employees not exceeding 250. These are the definitions used in this study.

national employment was also attributable to it. Moreover, there are certain characteristics of some members of the small-firm population which make this form of organisation particularly crucial to national economic performance. While fast-growing small firms represent a small proportion of the class, somewhat under 10 per cent, they do make a highly significant contribution to job creation (see Storey, 1994, Ch. 6). This employment feature is enhanced by the natural antidote which small-firm creation potentially provides to recession and unemployment, as more new firms are born from the larger pool of unemployed (Storey, 1994). Finally, while the small firm is less likely than its larger counterpart to have staff specifically devoted to research and development (R&D) activities, it is more likely to be innovative in its internal processes and outputs and thereby to initiate microeconomic changes which, in due course, will combine to generate positive macro effects on sector growth (Pavitt et al., 1987).[4] As Acs and Audretsch (1988) have put it, the 'new learning' in industrial organisations is that small firms are more flexible and innovative than larger firms. Thus, on grounds of both economic magnitude and importance in the generation of economic prosperity, a strong case can be made for focusing on the small firm.

However, in recent years empirical research in management accounting has been dominated by the study of current practice in leading Western and Japanese companies (e.g. Cooper, 1989; Monden and Hamada, 1991; Anderson, 1995). The capacity of such large firms to resource the development of 'best practice' through novel techniques, such as activity-based costing, target costing, balanced scorecards and throughput accounting, has attracted great research interest and this has become a major means of dissemination for these techniques. Implicit in this type of research is the belief that the discipline of management accounting is best served by studying (and so eventually facilitating the emulation of) the largest and most successful subjects (Kaplan, 1994). In comparison with this type of research, the study of management accounting in the small firm appears to offer little. It is unlikely that this type of firm possesses the expertise or the resources to develop significant practical breakthroughs or innovations in management accounting. However, the small-firm setting offers research possibilities and opportunities of a different type which are, nevertheless, of great importance to an explanation and understanding of the development and practice of management accounting *per se*,[5] and of its pervasive role in the economy. Indeed, much of the research potential of small firms derives directly from the contrast which they provide with the large organisation as a research setting. Some of the most significant potential advantages of the small firm as a research subject are outlined below.

---

4 For a more extensive examination of the relationship between micro behaviour of the small firm and its macroeconomic links, see Acs et al. (1999). See especially the paper by Davidson et al. (1999) who show, based on Swedish data, that even in the deep recession of 1990–3 small firms were a very important source of new jobs in Sweden.

5 As large firms were often originally small firms. An exception to this could be a small firm created by divestment of a component or unit within a large firm, a process sometimes described as 'disintegration'.

- The size of the small firm provides a relatively less complex research object compared with that of the large organisation. Consequently, within the small firm the nature, role and development of management accounting are more visible to the researcher.
- This enhanced visibility is combined with the susceptibility of the small firm to key contingencies such as the phase of the business lifecycle, high growth rates, financing issues and the extremes of competitive pressure (Garnsey, 1998). These influences are so prominent that a good location is provided for the study of the effects of these fundamental forces on internal accounting systems. Indeed, it has been argued that the key characteristics of small firms which differentiate them from larger organisations relate to uncertainty, innovation and their pattern of evolution (Wynarczyk et al., 1993). The structure of small firms is also more likely to be in a state of change as growth occurs in the small firm (Storey, 1994, p. 12). All these factors add to the potential value of the small firm as a management accounting study site.
- Prior research (e.g. Raymond and Magnenat-Thalman, 1982; Holmes and Nicholls, 1989; Nayak and Greenfield, 1994; Lybaert, 1998) indicates that the quality of management accounting information available within the small firm has a positive association with its performance. A refinement of this simple association is the view of Gul (1991) that the positive effect of sophisticated MAS information on performance will itself be higher, the greater is the perceived environmental uncertainty. The direct significance of management accounting in this research setting is thereby established.
- In new and young small firms it is only the birth and early years of management accounting systems that are observable. There has been a neglect of research focusing on the dynamics of this formative stage in the evolution of managerial accounting systems.
- The absence, in many instances, of professional or even experienced accounting support in the small firm inevitably limits the technical sophistication of internal accounting. This also means, however, that the management accounting which is found within this type of small firm will be derived purely from managerial needs and demand. The 'producer' or supply-side influence of the accountant is absent from the subject of study and consequently the small-firm setting will frequently provide a relatively pure and unique insight into the changing nature of management needs for accounting information.

For all the above reasons the small firm is potentially an extremely important research object for the management accounting researcher. It offers a basis for a derivation of the description, explanation and thus ultimately an understanding of the fundamental factors which influence the genesis and the development of management accounting in an organisational context. Indeed, the three theories used as a research framework (and outlined below) are based on the creation and form taken by the firm. Consequently, they provide one important rationale for the role of information (including management accounting) in an organisational setting.

1.3 Contingency theory

Contingency theory was developed as a means of explaining observed differences in the structure of organisations. It suggests that there is no unique best way of structuring an organisation under all circumstances. Thus a variety of contingencies will constitute the conditions appropriate to a particular type of organisation structure. Early research of this type suggested that environmental conditions, e.g. technological uncertainty (Burns and Stalker, 1961), and the technology employed by the firm, e.g. type of production system (Woodward, 1958, 1965) were key contingent variables. Further contingencies were suggested by Chandler (1962) (corporate strategy adopted), Lawrence and Lorch (1967) (market environment) and Otley (1980) (corporate objectives).

The contingency theory framework was adopted as an important basis for management accounting research in the 1970s. Rather than focusing on the organisational structure, this research was focused on the management accounting system. Indeed, the organisational structure itself was considered a management accounting contingency. Studies were primarily empirical and designed to ascertain which contingencies best explained observed management accounting practice. Burns and Waterhouse (1975) found that budgeting practice was influenced by the organisation's autonomy, the centralisation of its management and the uncertainty associated with the business as reflected in the degree to which key activities were structured. They concluded that 'a decentralised and structured organisation operating in a stable organisational environment seems particularly well suited to the use of budgetary control'. Hayes (1977) examined how management accounting practices differed across different sub-units within an organisation. His work suggested that the nature and significance of management accounting information was affected by the prevailing mix of three contingent variables within the firm: sub-unit interdependence (high in R&D); dynamism of environment (high in marketing); and internal characteristics such as work method specification (high in production). This use of contingency theory to explain intra-organisational differences in management accounting was extended by Waterhouse and Tiessen (1978) who argued that different parts of the firm would be affected in different ways by (possibly different) contingent variables. Thus managerial sub-units (concerned with planning and control) should be distinguished from operational sub-units (concerned with processing work). The former is more influenced by environmental factors affecting levels of uncertainty and the latter is more influenced by technological factors. Some implications of this situation for management accounting were tentatively explored. For example, high levels of uncertainty favoured decentralisation and in terms of control systems one would then expect high levels of participation, a focus on resource allocation mechanisms and a close monitoring of outputs. In contrast, where a production process is both familiar and stable, information targets can govern inputs and processes as well as outputs, and budgets can therefore be imposed with less participation.

In a more normatively oriented analysis, Gordon and Miller (1976) hypothesise that a firm's accounting information system will largely be determined by environmental and organisational factors and by the decision-making style adopted. They suggest that these contingent variables often cluster in three ways which give rise to three different firm typologies: the adaptive firm (a dynamic environment requiring analytical decision-making and a decentralised structure); the 'running blind' firm (also a dynamic environment, but requiring intuitive, entrepreneurial decision-making and a centralised structure); and the stagnant bureaucracy (a stable environment with conservative decision-making involving little analysis and a centralised structure). The management accounting best suited for these firms would vary in respect of the range of information provided, the need for lateral and vertical information flows, the speed with which information was provided, and the extent to which environmental information was included. Jones (1985) proposed an additional contingent variable when he examined the applicability of contingency theory to management accounting in conditions of organisational change (where a takeover has occurred) and found that the parent company became a major influence on the new subsidiary's management accounting. More recently Chapman (1997) has suggested that uncertainty (in respect of both objectives for, and consequences of, action) can be an intervening variable which influences the response of internal accounting to external contingencies and explains the relative inconsistencies found in many prior studies. Finally, an extensive review of prior research on how the contingency of selected strategy influences control systems has been conducted by Langfield-Smith (1997). Figure 1.1 summarises the basics of contingency theory as it has been applied to management accounting.

Figure 1.1: An overview of the contingency theory of management accounting

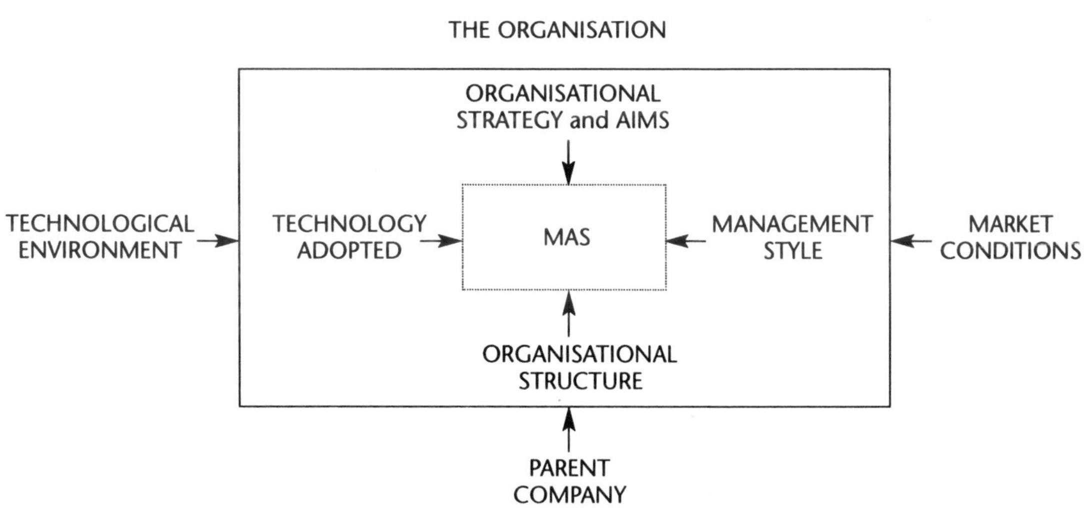

The basic premise of contingency theory – that a management accounting system is likely to be influenced by the circumstances in which it is designed and used – is little more than common sense. However if the 'circumstances' can be specified in a way which allows the identification of 'types' of firms which approach management accounting similarly, then a means of identifying a conditional set of 'best practice' is obtained. Differences in practice can therefore be explained and this intelligence used in the design of new, or the modification of old, management accounting systems. Moreover, the identification of contingent variables provides a useful insight into the fundamental factors which shape and influence management accounting practice. It does, however, explore these factors in a static rather than a dynamic fashion. Contingent variables are associated with accounting at one point in time. How these variables are implicated in change over time is not addressed. Otley (1980) points out further limitations of the contingency theory approach. The definition and measurement of both contingent variables and the management accounting system lack precision and general acceptance by different researchers (which reduces the value and comparability of findings). Furthermore, the nature of the relationships between contingent variables and management accounting is not well specified. For example, do environmental variables interact directly with the internal accounting system or does their influence occur through the organisational structure? In addition, is it possible that management accounting itself may be an influence on organisation structure rather than being purely a dependent variable? The specification of all relevant contingent variables is problematic. As Otley (1980) observes, the omission of important factors, such as the organisational objectives of the organisation, may distort the empirical results. Establishing a link to objective achievement or effectiveness is also desirable in order to identify the characteristics of management accounting systems which are associated with organisational success.

1.4 Agency theory

Agency theory has its roots in economic theory and is based on the following principles (Jensen and Meckling, 1976):

> Agency theory – a contract under which one or more persons (the principals) engage another person (the agent) to perform some service on their behalf which includes delegating some decision-making authority to the agent. If both parties to the relationship are utility maximisers there is good reason to believe the agent will not always act in the best interests of the principal.

It is a theory (e.g. Reid, 1987a) which is based on the behavioural premise that people act in a way which serves their own self-interest. Moreover, they can hide some of their actions from others and are also prepared to act in a way which allows them to benefit personally to the detriment of others. Consequently, when people combine to work there is a danger or moral hazard that individual members may shirk, i.e. fail to work as hard as they could and/or personally consume benefits which would otherwise accrue to the whole team. They will obtain all of the benefits of consuming such perquisites, while the principal bears a proportion of this cost. The organisational answer to this danger is to have a residual owner (or principal) who is entitled to any surplus created by the team members (agents) after remuneration has been rendered. The theory therefore explains the existence and basic form of the firm. The principal has no motive to shirk and will seek to establish systems for monitoring and rewarding the team (Figure 1.2). These will be designed to encourage the work team (or organisation) to act in ways which are congruent with the principal's aims. In these ways the principal attempts to guard against the informational advantage possessed by the agent (who has a greater familiarity and local expertise in the area of work undertaken) over the principal (information asymmetry). This, coupled with the moral hazard position, presents a circumstantial problem for the principal for which an information system may provide some assistance. Within larger firms an extended hierarchy of principals/agents can be found stretching from the owner or shareholder through the board, top management, middle management and supervisors to shop-floor operatives. Although only the shareholder is the residual owner, each level in the hierarchy does, to some extent, have to be managed by personnel who have to act as principals to their immediate subordinates, all within the overarching framework of agency theory.[6]

Figure 1.2: The principal–agent relationship

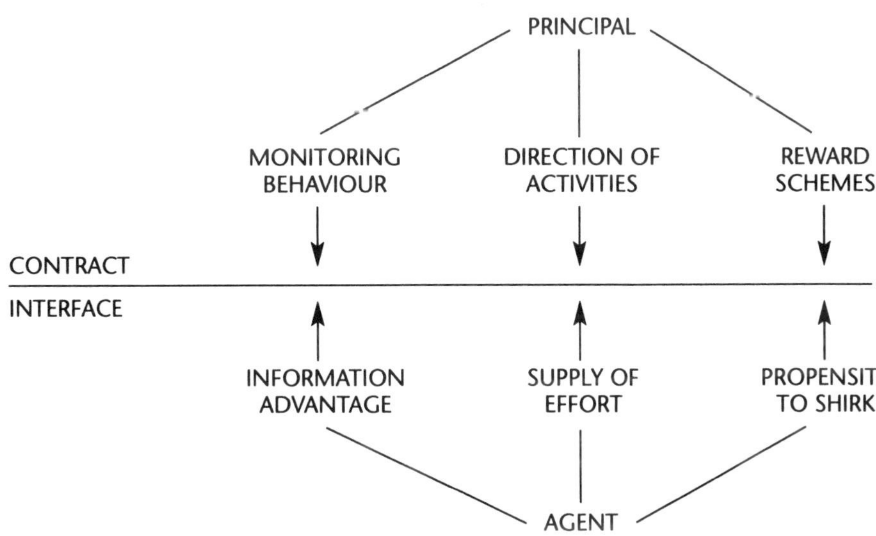

The application of agency theory to management accounting was initiated by the likes of Baiman (1982) and subsequently embodied in texts by Kaplan (1982), Ezzamel and Hart (1987) and Scapens (1991). The above conditions, existing within the firm, create a demand for management accounting information. The need to monitor and control agents' behaviour requires a flow of information from the relevant entity

6 Other applications of this framework are multifarious. An example related to the framework being explored here is the investor–investee relationship between the venture capitalist (as principal) and entrepreneur (as agent), as explored by Reid (1998). It is shown how monitoring permits the seeking of risk-sharing benefits without the sacrifice of effort. Further, it is shown that, as information becomes more reliable, an entrepreneur not producing effort can be induced to prefer to produce effort (Reid, 1998, Ch. 4).

to the principal. Accounting measures of actual performance, financial analyses of decisions, budgets and financial plans may all contribute to the provision of a basis upon which agent performance can be assessed.

The availability of appropriate financial controls and decision support can also be viewed as helping to direct the agent's behaviour in accord with the principal's interests. In addition, if incentives such as agent remuneration or even agent retention or promotion in employment decisions are to be based on performance, then management accounting may play an important role in providing information on the financial dimension of that performance. To play these roles, accounting has to be accepted by both principal and agent and should therefore possess sufficient 'hardness' and reliability to reflect an agent's actions adequately.

Agency theory also suggests that management accounting will be influenced by a variety of factors relating to each specific principal/agent relationship:

- The greater the divorce between ownership and control (which may mirror the size and complexity of the firm), the greater the need for information on the agent to be made available to the principal.
- The degree of incentive given by the agent's remuneration package – for example, where the agent's rewards are heavily based on performance which matches the principal's aims, the need for monitoring information (as a surveillance and control function) will be less.
- Conversely, the more sophisticated is the monitoring system in place, the less will be the need for the principal to base the agent's remuneration on performance levels achieved.
- The greater the complexity and uncertainty associated with the agent's role and work, the greater the information asymmetry which exists and the more the emphasis will have to be placed on monitoring inputs and outputs as opposed to processes.
- Changing management accounting will be a process of interest to both principal and agent and may involve protracted negotiation, given the sensitivity of its relevance to the relationship between them. Its establishment over time as part of the principal/agent relationship may deter change.
- The understanding of the persistence in use of apparent management accounting practice which is overtly less than generally accepted 'best practice' can be facilitated by an agency perspective. For example, Zimmerman (1979) contains an agency-based explanation of the practice of full cost allocation.

Agency theory therefore potentially provides a basis for improving understanding of, and for making predictions (as opposed to assertions) about, management accounting. However, the theory remains at a fairly high level of abstraction and the main findings from it (in respect of accounting) are rather apparent or obvious. The basic assumption of the pursuit of narrow self-interest may be questioned (e.g. on the basis of professional ethics which rise above such motives). The danger of moral hazard due to the agent's motivation for the consumption of perquisites may be attenuated by the existence of the labour market and the threat of the under-performing agent being replaced. Whistle-blowing by lower-level managers on their supervisors may also be an inbuilt safeguard against perk consumption, as may the threat of takeover by others who may be better able to cope with the threat of moral hazard. While generating many general implications for management accounting, agency theory does not readily lend itself to direct testing within an organisation.[7] In its present form it primarily provides insights (as opposed to easily testable hypotheses) into how economic factors respond to variations in risk and information provision within the context of the process of organisational evolution.

1.5 Markets v. hierarchies

The title of this theory contains the two options for the organisation of economic activity with which the theory is concerned. It is attributable to the work of Williamson (1970, 1975, 1992) and Coase (1937, 1990) and again it is a theory based on the economic motive. In essence it provides a rationale for the emergence of the firm. When activities conducted by separate individuals operating in the marketplace become voluminous, uncertain and complex they eventually reach a stage where they are relatively too expensive to undertake in this way. In other words, transaction costs become too great and the market fails to provide the most economic option for organising business. On balance, work can be more economically arranged by internalising its co-ordination within the framework of a firm. 'On balance' is mentioned because firms too may suffer from functional problems. At any time, it is necessary to determine which of the alternative organisations is transactionally more efficient.

Figure 1.3: The hierarchy option

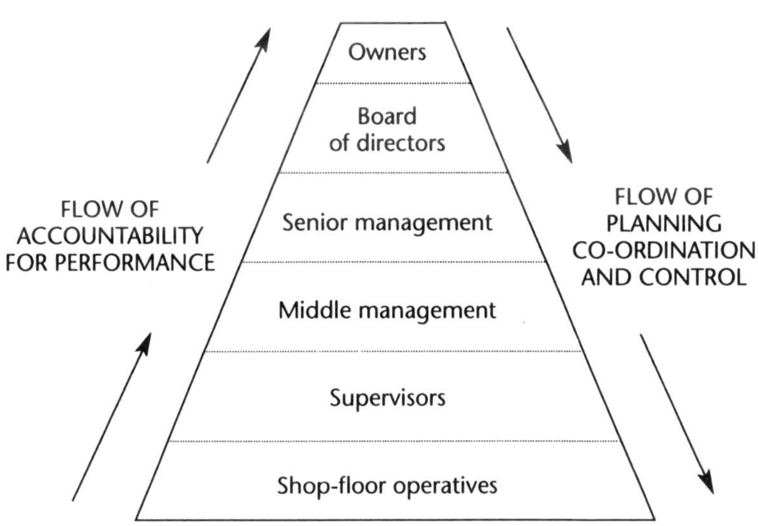

7 The approach therefore explored by Reid (1998) is to take a highly detailed look at implicit contracting practice from the standpoint of both principal and agent.

Within the firm a hierarchical structure (Figure 1.3), typically of pyramid form, provides a mechanism which promotes planning and co-operation and facilitates a control, order and direction which supplants the market on economic grounds.

Johnson (1983) and Flamholtz (1983) describe and debate this type of development from a historical perspective. They note how the change from a 'putting out' system arranged by the individual entrepreneur to the creation of the firm results in a demand within the new firm for financial information which was previously generated spontaneously by the market. For example, cost information about the production process provides a basis for management to assess the significance of its component activities and provides intelligence relevant to the pricing policy for final outputs. However, the theory also suggests that, as firms develop, their internal hierarchies will alter to better suit a range of variables, including their size, geographical spread and range of specialities. The demand for management accounting as a basis for co-ordination and control will emerge as part of the 'visible hand' which facilitates the organisation of business. Thus, as the hierarchical levels are created and increase within firms, and/or multi-divisional structures appear and grow, the need for budgetary planning and control becomes greater, and the need to translate aims and targets down the hierarchy also becomes stronger.

This can be done in financial terms (e.g. the use of return on investment (ROI) as a basis for divisional performance measurement). Moreover, there is a need to have information systems which distribute information among decision-makers in the larger, decentralised organisation, so that information impactedness (the tendency for economic agents to strategically commandeer information or resources for personal rather than organisational benefit) does not result in localised sub-optimisation. The competition engendered by firms, coupled with ownership expectations, will also promote internal searches for ways of improving the financial return. Systems such as management accounting will be designed to assist in locating such gains.

Within the hierarchical firm one of the most important factors in its operation is the internal labour market, and here too a demand will be created for management accounting information (Tiessen and Waterhouse, 1983). For example, in planning, the system will be expected to provide a means of sharing and distributing 'local' knowledge which will be of benefit to the organisation as a whole if widely known. In budget preparation, realism in statements of resource needs will affect the use of labour resource as a key building block for the successful use of the budgetary control system. The performance assessment of employees will also in many instances be, to a degree, dependent on financial information. This will influence the internal labour market directly, through the decisions made on remuneration rates for individual (or classes of) employees and the promotion, retention or releasing of them. Management accounting therefore becomes an integral part of the evolution of the organisation's hierarchy and plays a role in many of the most sensitive personnel issues raised within the organisation. For this reason any extant system (with some history in the firm) can be viewed as possessing a familiarity to, and acceptance by, organisational members. This places it in a strong position with regard to its continuity. Change in such a system will require a lot of consideration by and negotiation between employees before any agreement occurs. Technical accounting deficiencies may not be a sufficient justification for change, which will be a complex and potentially difficult process.

Although directly concerned with organisational control and administration, the markets and hierarchies theory also lacks specificity in the implications which can be derived for management accounting. It is suggestive of the basic need for internal accounting and the broad roles which it might play in areas such as planning, communication and employee assessment. However, it does not provide a basis for explaining or predicting differences in the details of observed practice. Its guidance is therefore once again broad, but it does highlight the dynamic nature of the creation and development of the organisational hierarchy as a key factor which will influence internal accounting.

1.6 Applying the theories

The above theories all focus on providing a rationale for the existence and/or the nature of business organisations. Consequently, it is hardly surprising that they provide an insightful theoretical basis for understanding the role and development of management accounting, which will normally be a major constituent of the organisation's information system. While each of the theories is distinctive, they can also be viewed as supportive and complementary as opposed to competing theories (Tiessen and Waterhouse, 1983; Ezzamel and Hart, 1987; Scapens, 1991). Contingency theory identifies many important contextual factors which relate to the operation of both the agency and markets and hierarchies theories. Hierarchical organisation structures may differ considerably and contingent variables (e.g. technological complexity and market competitiveness) may well help to explain these differences. Moreover, the mechanics of hierarchical relationships (between principals and agents) are the subject of agency theory which therefore provides one explanation of how organisational hierarchy structures operate. Many contingent variables represent a way of specifying the degree of uncertainty which impinges upon an organisational setting. The influence of this condition within the organisation may be reflected in the type of monitoring behaviour found in the organisation. For example, where *ex ante* uncertainty is high, less reliance may be placed on initial budgets, and budgetary revisions may be more common. Where *ex post* uncertainty exists on the attribution of outcomes, financial performance reports may be used in a more reserved manner, with more emphasis being placed on other non-accounting evidence to help triangulate the validation of interpretations of the information. Management accounting may therefore play an important part in smoothing the operation of the internal labour market by governing the interaction of people within the organisation. Its role thus becomes constitutional in relation to principals and agents operating in a hierarchical internal structure.

Above all, however, it is particularly apparent that the primarily static analysis of contingency theory (the association of management accounting with contingent variables at one point in time) is complemented by the dynamic nature of agency and market and hierarchies theories (which focus on the processes by which circumstances and relationships develop over time to facilitate organisational emergence and growth). These characteristics mirror the twin characteristics of this study. First, from a static perspective to examine the relationship between various aspects of management accounting practice and a range of contingent variables drawn from the above theories (e.g. age, size, structure, market, technology etc.), both individually and in clusters. Second, from a dynamic perspective to investigate whether changes in contingent variables give rise to changes in internal structures, relationships, processes relevant to agency and markets and hierarchy theory and ultimately to management accounting. Some of the key situational constituents and scenarios (which are also important components of the above theories) which are relevant to these theories, and hence to this research study, are briefly outlined below.

Organisational structure and ownership

- The reduction in the owner-manager's ability to monitor on a first-hand basis as growth occurs.
- The dilution of the owner-manager's stake in the business as external funding is introduced.
- Preparation for possible flotation on a junior stock market.
- The emergence of a middle-management tier.
- The initial creation of an internal (management) accounting unit.
- Various forms of organisational segmentation.

Economic circumstances

- The entry into new markets.
- The experience of financial difficulties and the pressure to ration capital.
- The development of technology employed.
- Rapid growth in size.
- The movement from single to multiple products and the introduction or cessation of specific product lines.
- The development of research and design capabilities.
- The facilitation of internal labour markets.

Information provision and use

- The genesis of management accounting systems.
- The emergence of specific components of management accounting such as product costing, budgetary controls, short- and long-run decision support information.
- Relative degree of reliance on *ex ante* and *ex post* accounting reports.
- The development of syntactical rules for accounting information production.
- The internal roles of accounting information and perceptions held of information 'fairness' and 'hardness'.
- Information use in high/low, uncertain and/or complex situations.
- Information as a moral hazard safeguard.
- The constitutional role of accounting.

1.7 Conclusion

The small-firm setting provides a particularly appropriate context in which to assess the consistency of the theories outlined above with observed practice. Within the small firm, key theoretical variables such as changes in ownership, structure, management, operations and markets interact in a formative manner with the creation and development of internal accounting. The small scale of the firms examined makes these factors not only more significant but also more visible to the researcher. Fundamental questions on why management accounting exists and changes, the form which it takes and how it contributes to organisational performance can be addressed. The abstract nature of these theories does not facilitate research of a detailed prescriptive type, but it does provide a framework to gain insight into the real-world rationale of practice (Mitchell et al., 1995, 1997). In achieving this, it is hoped that the identification, explanation and understanding of the real-world roles of management accounting can be enhanced.

2

Information and the Small Firm

2.1 Introduction

The theories reviewed in the preceding chapter provide a broad contextual framework for studying the emergence, development and use of management accounting in organisations. However, an understanding of the practice of information provision in small firms can also be enhanced by reviewing previous small-firm-centred work undertaken on the need for information, its role in decision-making, its suggested prescriptions and its significance for operational performance of the firm. This is the aim of the present chapter.

It is clear that small firms are under particular pressure to make accurate decisions, given the competitive conditions under which they typically function. Central to decision-making, especially if it takes place under pressure, is the set of information on which decisions are predicated. As Casson (1994, p.136) put it, 'accurate and relevant information is a resource'. The scale, scope, quality and timeliness of information have a crucial bearing on the decisions owner-managers make. Indeed, one can treat the role of information in terms of business strategy itself, as do Chang and Jevons Lee (1992).[1]

The early stages of the young firm's life cycle can be particularly turbulent, denying the owner-manager the comfort of settled circumstances in which little change is taking place. Rather, the dynamics of small-firm inception and growth mean that operational conditions are subject to rapid change. Even strategic goals may need to be flexible, and well adapted to evolving conditions, if the small firm's continued existence, let alone commercial flourishing, is to be guaranteed. Thus the informational requirements for good decision-making in the small firm are complex and adaptive. An important component of a modern information system within the small firm is the management accounting system (MAS).[2] This chapter initially sets the scene quite broadly concerning information in small firms, but then focuses progressively more closely on the managerial accounting perspective.

---

1 In their case, modelled formally as two differentiated oligopolies, the strategic weapons are information collection and volume of product or service.

2 With the notable exception of Jordan (1989), there has been little analysis of formal relationships between the economics of information and accounting information systems. Jordan's approach is to develop a transfer-pricing model of a management accounting system.

2.2 Information needs

In reporting on a study commissioned by the European Community (EC) into information system development for small firms, Trindade (1990) made reference to a number of key considerations. First, that the growth and success of small firms depended increasingly on reliable and timely information about market situations and opportunities, new technologies, industrial and commercial processes, as well as legislation and support schemes for enterprise. Second, typically there was within the small firm a lack of in-house expertise in developing information systems, which not only hampered the capacity to develop internally a system which was custom-built to serve the small firm's purpose, but also limited the capacity to evaluate and access available information systems of a generic sort that could, in principle, be adapted to meet, at least approximately, the small firm's unique internal needs. Third, and more positively, it was possible to use existing reliable and relatively low-cost information technologies to come some way to meeting the needs of the small firm. It was emphasised that such needs may have to be met by constraining the complexity of the information system, and above all by ensuring its cost-effectiveness.

At the time Trindade (1990) was writing, it was possible to point to a general lack of information relevant to small firms and their productive activities. More than this, on a conceptual level, no database structure seemed to exist which met the needs and potential of the small firm. In making recommendations about potential information systems, specialists in this field[3] emphasised early user involvement. The intention here was to encourage a self-consistent and operational approach, in which practical user experience developed along with new information systems (ISs). It was maintained that the fact that this involved use of sophisticated technologies should not be allowed to be an impediment to early user involvement. Rather, the recommended strategy emphasised the desirability of early user involvement. Not only would this place users on the learning curve as early as possible, but also their early presence would entail participation in the process of information system development itself.

The recommended approach referred to the rapid progress of computer technology, including powerful workstations and personal computers, which were becoming available at decreasing costs. To this were allied new types of applications software and network infrastructure which, although sophisticated, were increasingly user-oriented and friendly. The ultimate overall emphasis in this study (Ganzhorn and Faustoferri, 1990) was on distributed database management systems (DDBMSs). These run on both local and global levels, with the former only involving access at local sites, and the latter permitting privileged access to all data on all sites. While systems designed in this way have a wider significance to small-firm performance and development, they go beyond the immediate requirements of this book. Our small firms often do not have multiple sites for accessing information, and our narrower information class (management accounting information) allows us to take a more

3 At a conference which was an outcrop of this EC study.

restricted view. However, in due course, the DDBMS approach will no doubt become increasingly important to management accountants. Elements of this approach, and the demands for such services generated by accounting information system (AIS) development, are noted in the recent work by Jorrisen et al. (1997a).

Even if information systems development in small firms is perceived more narrowly than in Ganzhorn and Faustoferri (1990), one learns a lot from that work. For example, in developing an information system one needs to ensure that it contains information that is required, is usable, and is of requisite quality. Further, the system should permit maintenance of contact with the user in a fashion which is responsive to changing needs, and it should be constructed with an 'expert' human interface, i.e. an interface which permits easy access and meaningful interaction. Finally, cost considerations should not be ignored, in their scope and variety. In creating information systems, costs which arise include those of producing raw data, evaluating and validating data, entering data and retrieving data. Less obvious costs arise if measurement errors exist in data, some data are not available and some data are not used. Above all, perhaps, costs arise from maintaining the information systems. These include costs of updating information and system expansion and development.

Examples of the implementation of the Ganzhorn and Faustoferri approach are numerous. Gall (1990), referring to German experience, emphasised the encouragement of innovation within small firms. The aim was to boost innovative capability, from a situation in which many small firms lacked R&D departments. They therefore generated a demand for information on market developments and new technologies. In addition, they sought licensing agreements, patents and also valuable non-patented know-how, which was sold to the highest bidder. The solution to these information needs combined low and high technology. In a low-technology way, the Chambers of Commerce established a catalogue of innovations, each of which would be listed for two years.[4] This listed offers of, and demands for, new technologies. In a high-technology sense, this was supported by a distributed database system. This used industry-standard hardware and a widely available proprietary software package, specifically a relational database system. This permitted worldwide access on-line, and embodied useful user-friendly services like complete flexibility in German and English language input and output.

A second example, as recorded by Fang (1990), related to a national scientific and development plan in Shanghai. This area had over 1,000 enterprises, mostly small firms, mainly active in four sectors: mechanical processing; food and drink; textiles and clothing; and electrical appliances. A questionnaire indicated that 85 per cent of enterprises found information to be a valuable resource, but only 7 per cent had systematic ways of handling information. However, their information needs were extensive. Market information (85 per cent) and technical information (70 per cent) were ranked highest, but also significant were management information (34 per

4 This catalogue is questionnaire-based, contains thousands of entries, and the hard copy is computer-processed.

cent), personnel information (13 per cent) and financial information (18 per cent). The information network set-up needed to be appropriate to local conditions and was therefore simply fax machine based. These fax machines were linked by telephone and used to transmit mainly time-dependent data on market developments, material supplies etc.

Both of the above examples, by Gall (1990) and Fang (1990), illustrate how information needs can be met by exploiting positive network externalities. This aspect has perhaps been neglected in the literature, and indeed in information system development itself within the small firm. The latter is too often viewed in isolation from networks of various types, including the Internet, whereas it is apparent that greater efficiency and development would ensue were internal and external information needs to be genuinely interactive. For example, Jorrisen et al. (1997a) emphasise the need to access external information on such issues as industry trends, economic policy, new technologies, and so on.

Concerning the qualities which data relevant for decision-making within small firms should have, Zhiyou (1990) argues that information should be practical, detailed and relevant (e.g. to technological developments). Further desired attributes were that it should serve 'background' as well as 'foreground' purposes (i.e. it should facilitate scene-setting and suggest interdisciplinary connections, as well as meeting direct needs) and that it should provide a basis for further search (e.g. to usable secondary files or documents).

2.3 The use of information to guide decisions

Managers of small firms may partly be aware that informal systems of decision-making may be subject to bias. Thus unaided, intuitive decisions may be subject to distortions. They arise because our judgements and choices are sensitive to the way in which they are elicited. For example, judgements of market value of a company are known to be sensitive to the permitted form in which the response may be made (Slovic et al., 1990). When the response requires predicting the market value of a firm *per se,* the judgement elicited differs from that when the response requires predicting the firm's rank relative to the other firms in terms of market value. This difference arises even when the information sets of decision-makers are identical. Specifically, respondents in the former group tend to weight evidence on past market value more heavily, and those in the latter tend to weight evidence on past company rank more heavily, when predicting future market value or rank, respectively. In the case of valuing *small* firms, where publicly traded stocks are absent as devices for competitive valuations, biases of this sort can cause distortions in the absence of good information systems.

With regard to uncertainty, ways of dealing with it in the small firm may require an awareness that risk appraisal may not go so far as making a probability judgement. An example of making a probability judgement would be that there is a 10 per cent chance that the market extent for a new product will exceed £100,000 sales per annum, and a 90 per cent chance that it will be £100,000 or less. There may be a desire by the decision-maker to stop short of a probability judgement of this sort because the vagueness of the evidence only permits the appraisal that a large market is much less probable than a small market. Economists like Knight (1921) and Keynes (1921) were both aware that not all uncertainties could be gauged against the yardstick of unique probability distributions. To Knight, uncertainty appraisal made appeal to judgement or pattern recognition in essentially unique situations. Indeed, an intrinsic feature contributing to the uncertainty was that the situation had not been encountered before. By contrast, probability assignment made appeal to evidence on relative frequencies of similar, independent past events. Keynes argued that uncertainty concerning events came in three types. In the first, the information was so vague that events could not be compared; in the second, they could at least be ranked according to higher or lower probability; and in the third, actual numerical probabilities could be assigned. Despite a contemporary trend in risk analysis to advocate the use of number in risk estimation, a concession often made is that an indication should be given whether such estimates should be regarded as 'soft' or 'hard.'

Economists naturally suggest a cost–benefit approach to vague information. The costs of using non-numerical risk assessments are that the cutting edge in decision-making is lost, and advanced manipulation of probability statements (e.g. to compute compound or conditional probabilities) is lost. The benefits are that the decision-maker retains control by admitting that there are limits to the precision possible (e.g. by talking in ranges of possible probabilities, rather than point estimates) and is thereby more open to the context of the decision. For example, the decision-maker becomes more sensitive to features like the degree of dread of the downside, or the nature of risk which involves elements of the unknowable, because of lack of observation, time lags etc.). In fact, it is found that individual differences in understanding vague uncertainties are both reliable and substantial (Wallsten, 1990). Therefore, vague probabilistic forecasts may be preferred to precise ones, when that is all that the data warrant.

Of particular relevance to the growing new small firm is that area of decision analysis in which the decisions themselves are both dynamic and taken in real time. There are obvious analogies between running a new small firm and fighting fires, in a decision sense (see Brehmer, 1990).[5] First, a series of decisions must be made, not just one. Second, decisions are not independent. Third, the environment changes, both autonomously and as a result of the owner-manager's actions. While these attributes fully characterise dynamic decision tasks, the extra ingredient in the small-firm's case is that decisions are taken in real time. This has important implications. First, the decision-maker is not fully in control, and decisions may be forced. Second, decisions relate to processes, rather than events. Thus, actions need time to conceive and implement, and the timing of the implementations of actions itself is crucial – for example, it may only be possible in a window of time. Dynamic, real-time deci-

5 Indeed, Levy and Powell (1998, p.188), in an explicitly IS context, talk of small firms 'fire-fighting to deal with operational matters'.

sion-making shifts the perspective from the issue of *choice* of actions to *control* of the consequences of actions. Decisions are taken to control outcomes, and this requires a model of the systems to be controlled.

Control may be achieved by one of two strategies, feedforward or feedback. Feedback control chooses actions based on the current state of the system. Feedforward control involves choosing actions based on predictions about the state of the systems.[6] These controls help in dealing with real-time dynamic decisions. However, both have their problems. For example, feedforward control is less effective if the environment changes, and feedback control will not work if delays are significant.

In practice, decision-makers tend to favour feedback, rather than feedforward control. In terms of the heuristics of decision-making it is a simpler, less demanding method. However, if it does work tolerably, this may lead to the undesirable consequence that the decision-maker neglects possible benefits from a feedforward control system. In extreme cases, when delays in feedback are significant, the process may even be moved in a direction which is irrelevant to evolving events. On the other hand, feedforward strategies, to be successful, require both good observations on historical data for modelling purposes and relative stability of the environment on which to predicate the model's forecasts.[7]

Finally, Eliasson (1996) provides a caution against those who would place too much confidence in information systems within the firm. As small firms increasingly are knowledge based, and themselves function in what is becoming an information-based or 'weightless' economy,[8] so-called 'soft investments' within the firm become increasingly important. However, they are hard to incorporate in standard frameworks of monitoring, control and planning. By appeal to Simon's (1972) notion of 'bounded rationality' within the firm, Eliasson identifies four common biases in information systems:

1 This bias arises from missing items in the system. Notably, these are the 'soft investments' mentioned above. As the firm develops, there is an accumulating stock of product know-how, and employees learn on the job. Yet it may be that in knowledge-based firms these soft investments, being hard to quantify, play a lesser role in monitoring and control than they should. As a consequence, identifying the true source of profit may become difficult, and it may therefore be hard to exercise cost control appropriately in this area.

---

6 In an AIS development context, which is readily interpreted within small firm terms, Emmanuel and Otley (1986, p.260) say: 'the crucial feature is the provision of feasible feedforward controls ... without these, the provision of feedback controls, performance measures and budget variances is unlikely to lead to effective management control'.

7 The AIS can be turned to this issue. Thus Emmanuel and Otley (1986, p.263) say: 'the AIS has the role of scanning the environment to see whether the key assumptions remain valid'.

8 See work by Quah (1997) on the 'weightless economy'.

2 This bias arises from the measures adopted themselves. Here, the focus of Eliasson (1996) is on biased measures on the income side, notably of the capital gains part of profit, and also capital gains on inventory. These biases become acute during inflationary times.

3 This bias arises from excessive caution in discounting. A conflict can arise between enthusiasm for new product design and launch, and the desire for prudential financial management. The latter influence may react defensively against new product euphoria, often whipped up by technical staff, and this reaction may lead to applying excessively high discount rates to new product projects. Eliasson notes this bias and suggests decoupling new product investment decisions from the innovators within the firm. Putting these decisions in the hands of the chief executive places them beyond the over-reactive responses of the financial controller. This should help to limit excessive caution in discounting.

4 This bias in information systems arises from the adoption of wrong measures. Eliasson singles out for attention such measures as profit margins (instead of rate of return) and labour productivity instead of profitability. Eliasson (1996, p.147) argues, for example, that in investment contexts where decision-makers are unavoidably badly informed, a simple payback criterion can be 'an acceptable predictor of the rate of return'.

Concerning productivity measurement, Eliasson admits that it is relevant to performance appraisal where rates of return cannot be computed, but advises caution in its use, for fear that profitable opportunities for organisational change or new product development may thereby be neglected. In summary, Eliasson's misgivings about information systems relate to missing items, biased measures, cautious discounting and wrong measures. Though devised in a corporate context, this critique has obvious relevance to many features of small firm operations, in terms of information generation and utilisation.

2.4 The management accounting perspective

From the perspective of management accounting the extant literature provides little illustration of IS development within the small firm. Indeed, there is considerable evidence to suggest that within the small firm financial accounting has remained the principal source of information for its management (Carsberg et al., 1985). However, a variety of specialist publications on small-business management accounting is available. For example, Hollins (1983) adopts a sectoral approach, providing costing system guidance for small printing firms. Hicks (1992) adopts a technique specifically designed for applications within smaller enterprises, which is based on contemporary concepts of activity-based costing. However, the most prominent prescriptive guidance for management accounting in small firms within the UK is general in nature and comes in the form of monograph publications from three of its major professional institutes. These are reviewed overleaf, in an order which exemplifies the move away from a financial statement basis to a broader base which encompasses non-financial measures.

The first of these (Snow, 1967) focuses on the generation of interim accounts for the smaller manufacturing concern. This represents, in essence, a monthly reporting of the three key financial accounting statements (i.e. the balance sheet, trading profit and loss account and cash-flow statement). Some modification is made however, in addition to frequency, to their form for financial accounting purposes. First, they involve a direct comparison with and formal reconciliation to a set of forecast statements derived from the planned activity of the business. The reconciliation provided a specific recognition of where and how things were diverging from plan. Second, the inclusion of stock at its sales value, as opposed to cost, was advocated as a means of better representing the timing of profit generation month by month. An example of stock build-up then sale is used to demonstrate the advantage of this approach. This early realisation of profit might nowadays be criticised for lack of prudence. It does compound the dangers of motivating production for stock. A potential significance attaches to stock increases as a factor which may delay the recognition of profit decline (due to the carry-forward of fixed costs in stock). Third, detailed analyses of the business expenditures and dates when liabilities such as accruals fall due to be paid are made explicit, respectively, in supplementary schedules to the accounting statements and in the face of the balance sheet. According to Snow (1967, p.46), this will provide an effective system of financial control, particularly for the smaller business, which:

> (a) keeps the directors in close touch with the company's financial affairs, whether or not they are particularly skilled in financial matters;
> (b) keeps them informed from month to month on whether or not the company is achieving its targets;
> (c) does not involve the company in any exorbitant expense;
> (d) does not necessitate the engagement of any additional staff;
> (e) does not cause any inconvenience in the office or in the factory.
>
> For those concerns, large or small, which have full interim accounts in conventional form, the trading budget, cash forecast, and pro forma balance sheet provide an advance plan of the year's operations which gives their interim accounts infinitely more significance than if they were considered as a series of ad hoc exercises.

The Association of Certified Accountants (ACA) publication by Perry (1963) is also restricted by an emphasis on a financial accounting framework, as evidenced by the following introductory statement (p.7):

> The scope and objectives of management accounting need not make any extra demands on the accounting department of a business, because the figures moving through control accounts should be part of the day-to-day financial books.

Emphasis is placed on the generation of quarterly profit and loss accounts and cash-flow statements. These provide a detailed categorisation of all expenditures, though once again there is little support for any revenue analysis. The importance of budgetary comparison is highlighted with specific line-by-line identification and explanation of variances. This information is supplemented by the use of standard hourly rates (based on the budget) for both direct labour and production overheads. The actual expenditures of labour and production overheads for a period are compared with their 'standard recovery' (i.e. the standard rate times the standard hours worked). The resultant variances show whether work volume has been sufficient to recover these conversion costs fully from output. They therefore provide key managerial feedback on production performance. These standard rates are further used as a means of constructing price quotations for new work tenders. Perry (1963, p.35) concludes that:

> Management accounting is the one tool which can give to management the full opportunity of controlling a business in the areas in which real productivity occurs.

When this long-standing ACA text on IS development within the small firm first went to press, as discussed above, the world was a very different place in an information technology (IT) sense. Small companies typically did not have access to mainframe computers, desktop personal computers had not been developed, and advanced accounting software and related software (like spreadsheets and word processors) had also not been developed.[9]

The emphasis in Perry (1963) is on the productivity and profitability growth which are possible in the small firm if managers can reap the benefits of using the information which management accounting techniques can make available. Annual accounts (to determine profit or loss in a year) and in general audited accounts, prepared to meet statutory requirements (e.g. for taxation assessment), present the owner-manager with no more than a formal, historical picture of a business. Only by using accounting data for positive managerial control can the benefits of higher productivity and profitability be generated. Even if the macroeconomic situation, the stability of international markets and the phase of the national business cycle all bear heavily on performance, they are beyond the control of the small firm.[10] Nevertheless, within the small firm, control can be effectively exercised to utilise resources to their best purposes. This requires giving proper attention to analysing performance gains and losses associated with various configurations of financial gains and losses. In modern terminology, this is a feedback function. Further, it is necessary to have an allocation of responsibility for performance. This permits the setting of targets which

9 However, some small firms did have access to mainframe computer data processing services, and electromechanical and microelectronic desk calculators were available and had some programmed capabilities.

10 However, more modern views than those espoused by Perry (1968) would recognise that better awareness of external events can improve internal control.

may be checked against outcomes. In turn, this allows remedial action to be taken in the event of performance default. This is part of the feedforward function of an IS. Thus, systems developed in the small firm should facilitate both feedback and feedforward functions, to refer to previous terminology.

In focusing on the small firm, Perry (1963) is aware that a principle of parsimony must apply. Thus it is important to avoid imposing unnecessary tasks on those with accounting responsibilities within the small firm, especially at the time when an MAS is being installed or upgraded. Further, Perry (1963) advises against the clerical work becoming too complex (e.g. in allocating overheads to products or lines or sale). Rather, there should be proper management control of overhead expenses themselves. The principles of management accounting which should be adhered to in a small firm, according to Perry (1963, pp.8–9), are: the establishing of a profit target; the selection of budget periods; the establishing of the relationship between profit and cost control; the establishing of budget centres; and the valuing of time, seeking to determine a standard hourly cost. Variance measures the difference between allowed expenses at a cost centre and actual expenses, and is part of the feedforward system.

Perry (1963) argues that management accounts go far beyond conventional accounting requirements (conceived of in terms of audited sets of accounts) and, indeed, beyond the conventions of cost accounting. They enable a prescriptive approach to be taken to the organisation of any firm's accounting information systems. Prescriptions should aim to promote superior control, but only if it meets the end of increasing net profit.

The Chartered Institute of Management Accountants (CIMA) has recently collaborated with the International Federation of Accountants (IFAC) to produce a package of advice for small firms entitled *Financial Management Fundamentals* (IFAC/CIMA, 1998). This differs from the above two publications primarily in terms of its scope. While there is an acknowledgement of the value of regular internal management reporting based on conventional financial statements, the publication's orientation is to consider management accounting as a managerial component which must fit the overall business situation. Thus strategy, the market, firm capabilities, competencies and ambitions, are all key background factors which should influence management accounting. A general list of the types of information which might constitute the supply of management accounting is therefore provided as a checklist for consideration (Table 2.1).

The activities of planning and budgeting are again seen as central to a good small-firm information system, and it is suggested that a broad three-year look into the future should be accompanied by annual budgets prepared in advance of the year to which they apply. Moreover, it is suggested that the budget should extend beyond financial reports to non-financial indicators such as headcount, output levels and order-book situation. Indeed, the inclusion of non-financial measurements is a salient feature of this publication, with proposals that safety, quality, customer service, innovation, technology, distribution and administration could all be subject to this type of measurement. Cost analysis is also advocated, with information on cost variability considered beneficial for managerial decision-making and for the planning and evaluation of profitability through break-even analysis.

Table 2.1: Possible types of management accounting information relevant to small firms

Break-even point	Performance by product
Analysis of costs	Seasonal factors in sales, costs, purchases
Product costs	Order-book information
Monthly earnings	Key suppliers and customers
Actual revenue and expenditure (with budgeting comparison)	Trade amounts owed and owing (and timing thereof)
Non-financial indicators	Borrowings
Key financial ratios	Investment in fixed assets

Source: IFAC/CIMA, *Financial Management Fundamentals,* 1998

Two further areas of guidance are provided. First, a set of methods for small-firm managers to consider (Table 2.2). The financial information reviewed above can be considered a prerequisite for their successful use, as relevant information is needed to facilitate their adoption. Second, a 'do-it-yourself' toolkit is provided to exemplify the nature and presentation of information. Twenty-one items (Table 2.3) are included. For each, graphical illustration is provided to show how the item can regularly be monitored by management in ways which will give clear visibility to changes and trends appearing.

Table 2.2: Methods for small-firm management

Benchmarking	SWOT analysis
Debt factoring	Total quality management
Invoice discounting	Key supplier/customer identification
Just-in-time (production/purchasing)	Headcount ratio control

Source: IFAC/CIMA, *Fundamentals of Financial Management,* 1998

Table 2.3: 'Do-it-yourself' information topics

Funding structure	Return on sales
Cost of borrowing	Sales per customer
P&L – actual v. budget	Break-even calculation
P&L – annual component analysis	Contribution/break-even chart
Working capital	Production contribution and costs
Cash flow – actual v. budget	Contribution by product
Cash flow – projection	Market position
Capital commitments	Market share
Capital project cost control	Orders received
Utilisation of production facilities	Stockholding
Analysis of sales	

Source: IFAC/CIMA, *Fundamentals of Financial Management,* 1998

The prescriptive literature on small-firm management accounting is consistently based on a cycle of planning, budgeting and variance analysis based on a conventional financial statement framework. Recognition of the need to extend information beyond this base to include measurements of key intervening and output variables and key types of information for decision-making is apparent in the more recent suggestions. There is also the important recognition that small firms may vary in their accounting information needs, and consequently, while prescriptive publications can provide a menu of information supply, many situational factors, such as type of business, strategy, cost structure and market, will all influence the most appropriate management accounting package.

Finally, a more recent look at related issues of control of the small firm, reflecting a more IT-intensive environment, is the guide written by Jarvis et al. (1996). They focus on how small firms manage their cash flow and measure performance. It was found that within small firms owner-managers' self-determined objectives did not include growth, except in so far as it led to achieving a desired or an ideal size for the firm. Survival was the common goal, and success was measured by the attainment of a specific standard of living by the owner-manager. While cash-flow indicators were thought to be crucial, cash flow was often viewed in purely instrumental terms by the small-firm's owner-manager, in that it helped sustain the survival prospects of the firm. The notion of survival was itself thought to be complex and multidimensional. However, this apparent complexity and multifaceted nature of survival may divert attention from its more fundamental, and indeed simple, aspects. Thus, to many modern economists, long-run survival and profit maximisation are equivalent propositions. This is so because in competitive markets only firms which maximise profits can survive. Further, in progressively adapting operations within his/her small firm to promote survival against intense competition, the owner-manager is, in effect, incrementally moving towards profit maximisation.

2.5 Performance and AIS development

A general view of AIS development in the small firm would take as its starting point the stage of growth, or life-cycle position, of the small firm. Romano and Ratnatunga (1994) report on evidence on nine high-growth and nine low-growth firms in terms of the extent to which they adopted formal planning and control systems at various growth stages. They used a simplified three-stage growth model made up of:

- start-up growth, when informality prevails and control is maintained through operational involvement in the small firm, rather than formal processes;
- renewed growth, when formality increases, and planning and control systems are developed to handle internal, external and managerial issues;
- mature growth, when formality prevails, size and complexity are considerable, approaching the pattern of large corporate monopolies, and planning and control methods are fully applied to internal, external and managerial issues.

Three case studies were constructed, using fieldwork methods, for each of the three growth categories. It was concluded that the implementation of formal systems, of which the AIS is an example, was an important part of the evolution of the small firm. There was found to be a lack of concern with formal systems among low-growth firms which were experiencing either 'sustained' or 'steady' growth.

Typically, start-up small firms did not use sophisticated formal systems of planning and control, and as an alternative owner-managers tended to lean on their authority in running their firms. Traditional financial accounting for taxation and official revenue purposes featured heavily at this stage. Also important was the production of essential financial statements, like the balance sheet and profit and loss account. High-growth firms in this early stage were more likely to formalise systems, especially those for financial planning, partly for internal purposes and partly to attract and manage funds for future expansion.

In the second stage – of renewed growth – the low-growth firms tended not to use formal planning and control and did not look beyond the immediate future. Such planning systems as were used aimed to increase the efficiency of current operations, rather than seeking out and developing new business. By contrast, the high-growth firms at this stage had developed a more strategic approach to planning and control. They were concerned with finance, marketing and production, and these systems were integrated into the management structure.

Finally, in the third stage – mature growth – formal systems were widely adopted, but to different ends. Low-growth firms focused on technical efficiency, but continued otherwise to emphasise informal processes, and to bring personal influence to bear on operations. By contrast, high-growth firms used complex planning and control systems with skill and took a holistic view of the firm. Planning focused on resource development and the identification and adoption of new technologies, as well as on the maintenance of financial and physical operations.

Overall, the finding of this work by Romano and Ratnatunga (1994) is that formal planning and control is a feature of mature high-growth firms, and is less apparent in younger and/or lower-growth firms. The lifecycle evidence, that a commitment to more complex systems precedes subsequent high growth, suggests that at least part of the causality is from system development to performance.

A related picture is presented by Holmes et al. (1991), who talk of the information cycle of firms as corresponding to changing managerial roles as the small firm goes through its life cycle (e.g. growth, maturity). As the life cycle proceeds, so managerial functions alter. For example, in the growth stage 'developer–implementer' skills are to the fore, giving way to an emphasis on administrator–operator skills in the mature stage. Corresponding to these evolving managerial roles are evolving information system requirements. Thus, at inception, information levels are high because of a multitude of one-off information needs which must be met to get the business of the ground. These may be regarded as 'sunk costs'. As the business develops, information needs fall back to feedback levels for a while. Then, should growth follow, information needs arise again, to cope with complexity and dynamics, and to feedforward to the desired future form of the business. Another level may follow, at which the firm achieves maturity, and information needs again fall to a feedback level. This is the mature phase, which in time may be followed by decline, or – if adaptation is extreme – a further growth phase.

Each stage of growth requires an accounting information system appropriate to its features. Holmes et al. (1991) identify three levels of information complexity: ST, which is simply statutory information, typically for a government body like the taxation authorities (e.g. the Inland Revenue); SB, which is ST plus budgeted operation and capital information; and SBA which is statutory plus budget plus additional accounting information. Some information is internally focused, such as cash-flow statements, break-even analysis, production reports; and some information is partially externally focused, like interfirm comparisons and industry trends. The extent of information development is then treated as a variable to be explained by small-business attributes. Thus, the focus here is on how the firm's development generates a need for AIS development, whereas previously the focus has been on how AIS development 'feeds forward' to enhanced growth performance.

Holmes et al. (1991) put forward four hypotheses about the level of information: that it relates to age, to size, to sector and to managers' educational attainment. These were tested on a sample of over 900 Australian small firms using an ordered logit model. It is found that larger (growing) small firms require more information than smaller (possibly stagnant) small firms. However, older firms use less complex information than younger firms, and more standard information. The more educated the manager, the more likely were both SB and SBA to be used, as compared with simply ST (which had a declining proportional significance with education). The size effect, too, was marked, especially as regards SBA, which was much more widely adapted by larger small firms.

A related, earlier study is reported upon by Holmes and Nicholls (1989), using the same sample of data. They find that statutory information is largely prepared by external accountants, whereas additional information is prepared within the business. In the latter category one finds ratio analysis, manufacturing statements, interfirm comparisons, industry trends, source and application of funds, break-even analysis, cash-flow statements, production reports and job costing reports. In the last four categories the percentage of internal provision is very much higher than external provision. Their other results are as reported (in simplified form) in the later study.

It seems clear from these perspectives on information and the growth of the firm that information both determines and is determined by growth. The specific form this information takes has been explored by Jorrisen et al. (1997a, 1997b), where here they emphasise information use within a planning and control perspective, as in the work of Romano and Ratnatunga (1994). The causality is seen as running from planning and control to successful outcomes in terms of superior firm performance. Jorrisen et al. report on survey and case study evidence on small firms in Belgium. The evidence gathered consisted of 94 questionnaires and 38 company case studies. The split between successful and unsuccessful firms was approximately 60 per cent and 40 per cent, respectively, for the questionnaire sample and 50 per cent and 50 per cent for the case study sample. A good spread of small firms across size and sectors was a feature of these samples.

The focus in Jorrisen et al. (1997a) is on small firms *per se,* and performance differences across them, whereas in Jorrisen et al. (1997b) the comparison is between small firms and larger enterprises. Considering the earlier work first, the three areas investigated were planning, control and performance. All are integral to the small firm's 'information set'. It was found that most small firms did not have long-term plans, though larger firms were more likely to have them than smaller firms. For example, less than a quarter of firms with fewer than 20 employees had long-range plans, whereas over a half of firms with more than 50 employees had such plans. These long-range plans covered matters like marketing, production, personnel, R&D, investment and finance. The last two were generally the most significant components of long-range plans. Unsuccessful firms had a wider scope to their long-range plans than successful firms, with more attention being paid to production, personnel and R&D in particular.

As the earlier part of this chapter emphasised, external information may be as important as internal information to the small firm's AIS development. This is clear from the planning evidence referred to by Jorrisen et al. (1997a). Thus, as well as considering internal information for planning, such as sales, product quality, production and personnel, such small firms also looked at external information concerning general economic indications, industry trends, government interventions, new technologies, legal regime, and (to a lesser extent) money and capital markets. Moving from long-range to short-range planning, budgeting and cash flow were emphasised. The smallest small firms were far less likely (63 per cent) than the largest (20 per cent) to use budgeting. Of the budgeting methods used, the traditional form was most common, followed by flexible, zero-based and incremental budgeting.

Budgeting was more frequently used (about twice as often) in unsuccessful firms, but often later than required. Typically, budgeting was started because of financial problems. Focusing attention on the detail of budgeting and the sub-budgets within the master budget, it was found that sales, investment and cost received the most attention. Within the cost budget itself, indirect fixed cost was most important. Unsuccessful firms focused more heavily on production and cost, to the relative neglect of liquidity. The prime information source used for preparing budgets was historical data (typically taking figures of the previous year). Unsuccessful firms reported considerably greater difficulty with budgeting than did successful firms. For example, they worried particularly about missing or unreliable information, and were concerned about budgetary slack. The unsuccessful firms were also generally more aware than the successful firms of the potential advantages of budgeting. Thus unsuccessful small firms emphasised how budgeting improved co-ordination and communication, employee motivation and control. The main perceived advantage of budgeting by successful firms was that it confirmed their ability to take corrective actions.[11]

While budgeting is not popular in small firms, variance analysis is even less so, on the evidence of Jorrisen et al. (1997a). Although variance analysis is the archetypal

11 Cash-flow analysis was more popular with larger than smaller small firms, but generally not widely practised.

approach to management accounting, as far as financial control is concerned, only about a quarter of small firms used it. Sales price and sales value variances were by far the most commonly used, followed by labour efficiency variance.

In fact, financial ratio analysis was the most popular way of appraising financial performance, with the gross profit margin (two-thirds) being the most popular, followed closely by the net profit margin, and then (far less popular) the gross sales margin (about one-third), followed closely by the net sales margin. Less than one-fifth of these firms used the return on assets as a financial ratio. Although unsuccessful firms compute these ratios at much more varied intervals than successful firms, the latter emphasise a limited range of intervals, e.g. annual and quarterly reporting, but report more heavily at these dates.

A wide range of non-financial performance indicators was also used by these small firms. Most were administrative indicators (e.g. timeliness and accuracy of invoices), and innovation appeared to be relatively unimportant. In terms of the sample split between successful and unsuccessful firms, the latter were markedly more oriented towards customers, administration and innovations. The successful small firms seemed able to take customer interest for granted, and they emphasised production, sales and administration, and also internal business processes and management decision-making. The unsuccessful firms were struggling at a prior level, emphasising customer perspective, after-sales service and innovation, but apparently with fewer consequences. In terms of 'benchmarking', too, unsuccessful firms are more active here. Benchmarking was widely interpreted and implemented. Typically, it was treated as assessing the relative price and quality of rivals' products, mainly through using business magazines.

Overall, this major work by Jorrisen et al. (1997a) indicates that relatively unsuccessful small firms often used a more varied repertoire of planning and control techniques and adopted more intensive (and frequently more sophisticated) techniques than their more successful counterparts. Thus, they generated more complex demands for information system development. It was found that short-term planning and especially budgeting were more used in unsuccessful small firms. In a related study by Jorrisen et al. (1997b), it was found that large companies differed from small firms mainly in their successful use of long-range planning. Their general conclusion is that 'planning and control are not necessary tools for success, but they do become necessary when firms are facing difficulties and when firms exceed a certain size'.

In the work of Nayak and Greenfield (1994), a sample of two hundred micro-firms was examined in 1990 in terms of their accounting information systems. The great majority (89 per cent) had not found accounting difficult. At that time (1990) only a quarter used a computer, the owner-managers typically did not write up their own books, and in nearly a half of the firms the books were written up daily. Most (91 per cent) kept a cash book and nearly all (97 per cent) knew their bank balance. Generally, the smaller and less well-performing firms had the least adequate debtor records.

However, in considering the day-to-day monitoring of these micro-firms, Nayak and Greenfield (1994) found only about a third produced budgets, though, if they did, these were then used to compare budgets with performance. Nevertheless, most of the important data for monitoring were available in these businesses, notably sales, fixed costs, product costs and, usually, average gross profit (per cent). Calculations undertaken to monitor the firm were typically weekly (75 per cent), and the key data analysed were sales or profit. The poorer performing firms were found to be less likely to use budgets.

More detailed formal records were not widely used, with only about a third keeping production schedules or stock records. However, cash books and order books were common (about two-thirds) and a nominal ledger which went beyond creditor records was widespread (80 per cent). Generally, the firms doing less well had less detailed records. There was evidence that increased complexity of records was caused by growth, rather than the reverse.

Information for decision-making (e.g. as regards marketing and pricing) was also examined. Most firms (about three-quarters) did not have enough customers, and the pricing decision was found to be difficult, extending often to not knowing whether price should be reduced or raised. The less knowledgeable firms (typically younger, smaller and poorer performers) sought the most information on which to base their pricing decisions.

The capital investment decision was taken seriously by most firms, but often approached informally. Efficiency was the most commonly cited (about half) reason for capital investment, but arguments were rarely backed up by formal analysis. With young and/or small firms, necessity rather than efficiency was a more usual reason for capital investment.

The general finding of Nayak and Greenfield (1994) was that the less well-performing firms had more difficulty in using accounts, wrote up books less frequently, were less likely to prepare budgets, and kept records which had both a narrower scope and less detail than more successful firms. These results are somewhat different from those of Jorrisen et al. (1997a, 1997b), which indicate that struggling firms can have more complex and extensive information needs than successful firms. However, Jorrisen and colleagues were typically looking at larger small firms than Nayak and Greenfield (1994).

2.6 Statistical analyses of AIS and performance

Although a number of studies mentioned in the previous section make appeal to statistical evidence, this is very often of a descriptive, rather than inferential, nature. Further, it is generally used to develop, criticise or extend a variety of qualitative hypotheses about performance and the AIS. Here, by contrast, concern is explicitly with quantitative analysis, including appropriate inferences, and with confronting hypotheses in a quantitative, rather than qualitative, sense.

At the boundary between the two sorts of work is the study of Raymond and Magnenat-Thalmann (1982). Their concern was to refocus research effort in this area in a quantitative direction. The work was based on 218 questionnaire returns from a group of small firms (employment 20–250) in the province of Quebec. This sample was split into sub-samples of 129 and 89 small firms, depending on whether electronic data processing (EDP) was or was not used, respectively. The importance of various management decision problems was assessed, and then the satisfaction of owner-managers with their available information about these problems was ranked. In terms of differences between those firms that did use EDP and those that did not, there was no statistical significance in the help deriving from it, save in the preparation of financial statements.

The forms that EDP took were diverse, as regards applications area, with accounts receivable (85 per cent), payroll (79 per cent), accounts payable (77 per cent), general ledger (75 per cent) and sales analysis (75 per cent) being the most frequently present in small firms. Almost two-thirds used standard software packages, rather than packages which had been custom-built. The potential for interacting with computer-based information systems was not viewed very positively by owner-managers. Their perceived value, as decision support systems, was not great. Overall, the lack of impact of EDP led the authors to feel that the potential role for MISs in small firms had not been fulfilled. Rather, the impact seemed to have been in dispensing with many clerical operations, rather than in improving planning and control.

These results were perhaps to be expected of an era which emphasised the 'number-crunching' advantages of software systems, to the neglect of their managerial implications. In the work of Gul (1991), the use of systems within the small firm, specifically the MAS, was analysed in terms of its impact on managers' performance within small firms. The hypothesis explored was that the link between an MAS and performance was itself contingent upon perceived environmental uncertainty (PEU). In terms of contingency theory, Gul (1991) was aiming to explore the relationship between contextual variables and complexity. The MAS was calibrated in terms of four informational characteristics: scope, integration, timeliness and aggregation. Scope referred to the extension of information to external, non-financial and probabilistic areas. Integration referred to interaction effects between the small firms' functions. Timeliness referred to the frequency and speed of reporting. Aggregation referred to using analytical or decision models (e.g. discounted cash flow, inventory control), as well as combining data over time or functional areas.

The central hypothesis tested is that Y (performance) depends linearly on three terms: MAS, PEU and an interaction term measured by the product of MAS and PEU. It was predicted that Y and MAS would be positively correlated for large values of PEU, and negatively correlated for small values of PEU. Data were based on 42 questionnaires returned from small firms in Queensland, Australia.

Using the above model, it was found that the results of contingency analysis were supported in the sense that sophisticated management accounting systems contribute to performance under high perceived risk, but lower performance under low perceived risk. Under high risk, entrepreneurs feel that competitors' actions, market demand etc. are very unpredictable, so they use complex MASs to deal with such problems. Not only does this help them to 'put out fires', it also allows them to respond rapidly to new contingencies, utilising advantages conferred by a complex MAS, such as timely, frequent and high-quality information. On the other hand, when risk levels are low, a complex MAS is not justified. Indeed, it may be over-specification for the needs of such small firms, and could lead to dysfunctional behaviour (e.g. time wasting in learning about a complex system, as a goal in itself), with negative consequences for performance.

More recent work by Libby and Waterhouse (1996) supports the view that organisations working in more competitive environments tend to greater adaptation in their MAS. Indeed, this work in general would oppose views expressed by the likes of Levy and Powell (1998, p.193) to the effect that 'firms all exhibit relative inflexibility in their general approach. Information systems do not seem to provide increased flexibility, but reinforce existing thinking.' However, this work is based on a set of four case studies of manufacturing small firms, all confined within one region. Libby and Waterhouse (1996) base their analysis on data from 24 manufacturing firms in Ontario over the period 1991–3. Depending on what definition of size one adopts, the fraction of small firms in the sample was between a third and a half. Few very large firms were included. Multiple regression analysis was used to discover the relationship between changes to MAS and causal factors like decentralisation, size, competition and organisational capacity.[12] It was found that organisational capacity was the best predictor of change in MAS: there was a positive and highly significant association between these two variables. However, the decentralisation, size and competition variables were insignificant. A further regression was computed to explain change in the components of the MAS (specifically in directing, decision-making, controlling, costing and planning). Again, organisational change was the only significant predictor of this.

Probably most sophisticated in its use of quantitative methods is the recent work of Lybaert (1998). It examines 208 small firms in Belgium and, in general terms, finds a positive association between information use and performance. Lybaert (1998, p.171) notes that 'it is very astonishing that in this information age – in which the importance of information for everyone is so accentuated – there are so few profound studies on this process in the small firm'. Essentially, there are three 'hypotheses' explored by Lybaert:

- small firms that are better informed about R&D and rivals will have above-average performance;
- information use in the small firm will be positively associated with information awareness, educational attainment, lack of business experience, growth orientation and knowledge of administration;
- information use in the small firm will be greater, the larger is the firm, the earlier its stage, the less is family intervention, the more is delegation, the greater is the availability of ISs and the less are costs a problem.

All three hypotheses are accepted, though it is perhaps more accurate to say that these hypotheses represent the findings of a highly inductive approach to information use in the small firm.

12 Measured by the number of MASs that had been put in place by 1993.

The statistical method of Lybaert (1998) uses the so-called linear structural relations model (LISREL). It is a regression method, which aims to both measure and analyse relations between components of the system being examined. Data were gathered by questionnaires. The general finding was that greater information use in small firms was associated with better performance. The characteristics of the owner-manager and small firm which determined the extent of information use positively included: strategic awareness, newness in business, growth orientation, freedom from family intervention and strong delegation. Though there was no formal analytical model, there was a kind of schematic model. In it, information use and success were determined, with the latter leading to the former. The determining factors impinged directly on information use and were of two types: person-specific characteristics (e.g. personality, education); and firm-specific characteristics (e.g. maturity, size, availability of IS).

2.7 Conclusion

Table 2.4 summarises the key findings (reviewed above) of existing research on the relationship between information provision and the small firm. It reinforces the notion that information, including management accounting, is potentially an extremely important resource for this type of firm, impacting on both managerial effectiveness and firm performance. However, the analysis of information use in the small firm is in its infancy. Information needs can be analysed from a multidisciplinary perspective, and indicate that they hinge on the decision framework of the small firm. The management accounting perspective is useful in that it helps formalise the characteristics of an information system, and suggests how its design can best be directed towards monitoring and control functions which embrace performance.

The link between performance and AIS development has begun to be explored, but the field is new, and occasionally conflicting. While performance and information use are clearly linked, the relationship may be U-shaped, rather than monotonic. That is, low performance (the struggling firm) may generate relatively great IS needs. Further, the relationship may be sensitive to the life cycle of the small firm, with young firms having relatively high information needs.

Statistical analysis of the information use and performance link in the small firm extends the limits of modern research practice. Results are few and far between, and the data analysed are disparate, relating to different countries. However, they generally indicate a link between information use and performance, and suggest what characteristics of the small firm may strengthen this link, such as the experience, education and attitude of the entrepreneur.

Table 2.4: Summary of research findings on information and the small firm

Summary of findings	Research source
General information needs	
Growth and success of small firms depend upon reliable and timely information on markets, technology, legislation and available support, *plus* typical lack of expertise to develop systems, *but* information technology offers a solution if the system is kept simple and cost-effective	Trinadde (1990)
Advocacy of distributed database systems to support small-firm information needs	Ganzhorn and Faustoferri (1990)
Description of a central 'clearing house' listing offers of and demands for new technology, based on a distributed database and used in Germany	Gall (1990)
Description of a fax-based system of information on market developments and material supply availability in the Shanghai area	Fang (1990)
Decision-specific information	
Decision-making may be programmed and quantitatively based or more *ad hoc* and qualitatively, or even intuitively, based	Wallsten (1990)
Decisions often occur in complex, dynamic and uncertain conditions, especially in the small-firm context	Brehmer (1990)
Decisions and control may be based on a feedback (current state) or feedforward (future prediction) basis and, while the former is more convenient, the latter is more relevant	Emmanuel and Otley (1986)
Small-firm accounting information systems for decision support have four limitations: (a) 'goodwill' resources, e.g. know-how, are missing; (b) measurement – the neglect of capital gains on assets, including stocks; (c) excessive conservatism in the financial assessment of new product investment; (d) use of erroneous measures, i.e. not matching purpose	Eliasson (1996)
Management accounting prescription	
Suggestion of monthly reporting package based on balance sheet, profit and loss account and cash-flow statement, compared with forecasts and modified to reflect capital gains on stocks	Snow (1967)
Similar quarterly accounting package suggestion, with detailed expenditure breakdown and overhead recovery information	Perry (1963)
Suggested extension of accounting information to include many key success factors (e.g. product costs, order book position, non-financial measures) and analyses (e.g. SWOT, benchmarking comparisons) which would be regularly monitored	IFAC/CIMA (1998)
Emphasis on the importance of the survival objective and the relevance of cash flow	Jarvis et al. (1996)
Firm performance and accounting – non-statistical studies	
Accounting information becomes more formal and bureaucratic as firms grow in size. This is an important part of firm evolution	Romano and Ratnatunga (1994)
As the management role moves from the early stage 'developer-implementer' to 'administrator', so the accounting function needs change. Further influences on information include the firm age, sector and managerial education level	Holmes *et al.* (1991)
Successful firms have much more closely focused long-range plans. External information (e.g. industry trends, economic indications) was considered an important part of SME accounting system development; larger SMEs were much more likely to use budgeting, as were unsuccessful firms. Budgets were a reaction to financial problems	Nayak and Greenfield (1994)
Firm performance and accounting – statistical studies	
The use of EDP did not help in information support provision, except in the case of financial statements	Raymond and Magnenat-Thalmann (1982)
Sophisticated management accounting systems improve performance where firms operate in a highly uncertain environment, but are associated with lower performance in a low-risk environment	Gul (1991)
Organisations have greater change and adaptation in their management accounting when they operate in more competitive environments and exhibit organisational change	Libby and Waterhouse (1996)
Greater information use in SMEs is associated with better performance	Lybaert (1998)

3

Fieldwork: Sampling and Questionnaire

3.1 Introduction

The empirics of this study involve dual but mutually supportive strands of investigation. Initially, a statistical analysis of key small-firm and contextual variables drawn from an extensive sample of relatively young small firms was undertaken. This provided the basis for examining various aspects of small-firm management accounts in practice and for conducting a range of tests relating to the theories outlined in Chapters 1 and 2, and drawing from these some general conclusions. In addition, a series of three more detailed case studies were written using data gathered during four visits to three firms. These provide detail on the interaction of the factors studied on a statistical basis and allow a richer appreciation of the process by which management accounting emerges and develops in the small-firm context.

This chapter reviews the method used in collecting the data for this study. It comprises four substantive sections. First, the basis on which the sample of firms selected for study is described and the sample profile presented. Second, the design and application of the interview schedule is explained. Third, the incorporation of data gathered in a database, to facilitate analysis, is outlined. And last, the selection of subjects for the case studies is detailed and the range of evidence used in their construction is outlined.

3.2 Sampling

An aim of the study was to ensure regional diversity in the sample, which was achieved by stratification, without sacrifice of the benefits of random sampling, in terms of statistical inference.[1] Because there is no national register of start-up firms in Scotland, another source had to be found for the sample. The Enterprise Trusts were the natural choice, as they are often the first port of call for a budding entrepreneur seeking to start up a new venture. Enterprise Trusts place a strong emphasis on helping firms to grow and become more profitable concerns, for their own good as well as for the local economic community. The sampling procedure used had previously been successful in the study by Reid (1993),[2] and this established reputation facilitated access to the field.

1 See Sekaran (1992, Ch.8).

2 See also Reid (1987b), in which he describes in detail the methods he has used in his own previous research.

Following meetings with key figures in the enterprise community, who provided guidance on the sampling criteria, a random sample of eighteen Enterprise Trusts was utilised to provide the starting sample of 150 firms.[3] Table 3.1 details the regions in which the sample of small firms lay, and Figure 3.1 indicates the areas in which interviews were conducted. Thus the sample provides good coverage of the most densely populated areas of the country, ranging from as far north as Gordon Enterprise Trust in Inverurie, through the central belt of Stirling and Falkirk, down as far as Cumnock and Doon in the west, and Midlothian in the east. The procedure adopted was to ask directors of Enterprise Trusts to provide a random sample of firms on their client lists.

Table 3.1: Area covered by the study

Region	Enterprise Trust
Grampian	Gordon Enterprise Trust Aberdeen Enterprise Trust
Tayside	Angus Enterprise Trust Dundee Enterprise Trust Perthshire Enterprise Company Ltd
Central	Stirling Enterprise Park Alloa Clackmannan Enterprise Ltd Falkirk Enterprise Action Trust
Fife	North East Fife Enterprise Trust South Fife Enterprise Trust
Lothian	The Capital Enterprise Trust Midlothian Enterprise Trust
Strathclyde	Glasgow Opportunities Govan Initiative Strathkelvin Enterprise Trust Clydesdale Development Company Ltd Hamilton Enterprise Development Company
Borders	Cumnock and Doon Enterprise Trust

3 It should be mentioned here that the Highlands and Islands were excluded from the sample both for reasons of practicality (e.g. remoteness, financial constraints) and because the Enterprise Trust structure in this area differs quite significantly from that in the rest of Scotland. See, for example, Reid (1996), in which he reports upon the differences in funding shortages experienced between small firms in the Highlands and Islands compared with those in the rest of Scotland. Fife firms were used in the pilot.

Figure 3.1: Interview clusters (circles indicate the areas around which the interviews were clustered)

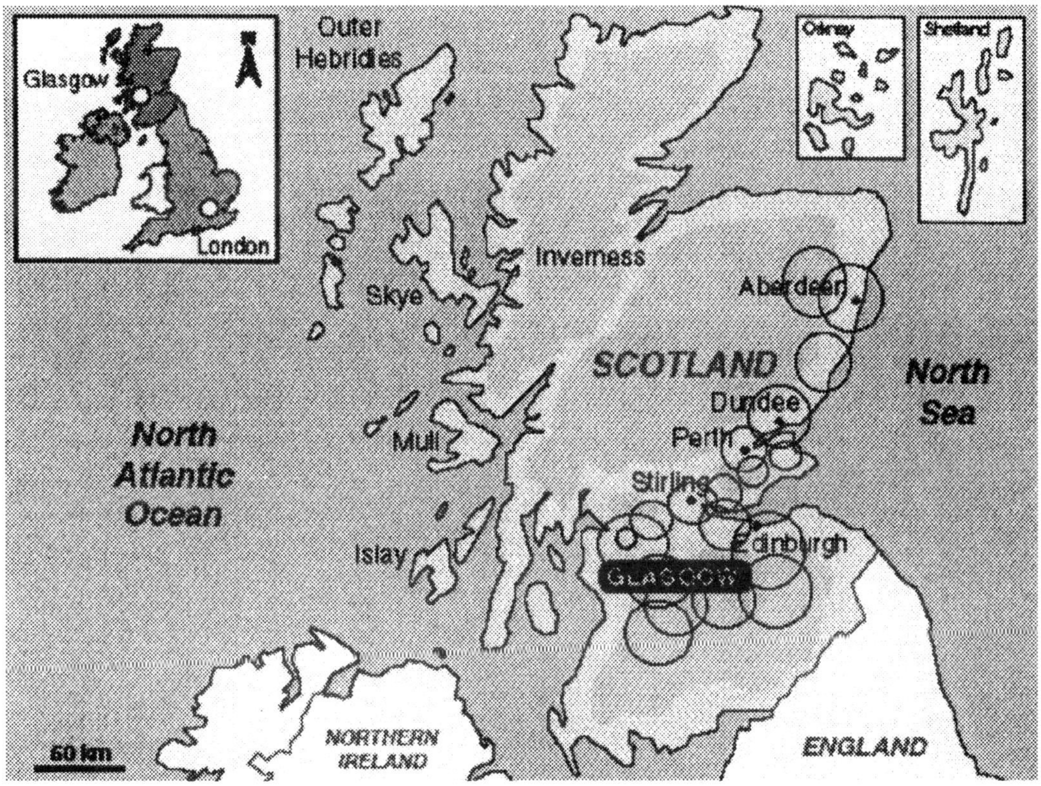

The only conditions put on this sample were that the firms should be less than three years old, and that they should have started up through the Enterprise Trust. The initial sample of 150 firms is certainly a sufficient number to constitute a statistically 'large' sample, as defined, for example, by small-sample distribution theory.[4] Recent figures released by Scottish Enterprise (1996) suggest that the sample corresponds very closely to the much larger picture of new Scottish firms in the 1990s. For example, by legal form, the 1993–4 sample used in this study comprised 26 per cent sole traders working from home, 29 per cent sole traders operating from business premises, 19 per cent partnerships and 27 per cent private limited companies. The Scottish Enterprise figures for 23,000 new firms in 1996 give sole proprietorships at 48 per cent, partnerships at 21 per cent and limited companies at 30 per cent.[5] The categories, although slightly different, show clearly that there is a high similarity of breakdown by legal form between the two samples.

4 From the perspective of the Student t-distribution, sample sizes above 70 are effectively 'large' samples.

5 Storey (1994) reports on the findings of Bannock and Partners, who calculated that, in 1986, for the UK as a whole, 55 per cent of small firms were sole proprietorships, 26 per cent partnerships and 19 per cent limited companies. By 1989, Daly and McCann (1992) found a similar breakdown of UK firms by legal form.

The division by sector is a slightly more contentious issue, but is nevertheless still worth addressing. Scottish Enterprise state that 68 per cent of new businesses in Scotland in 1996 were in services, compared with 64 per cent in this study.[6] Figures from the Department for Education and Employment (1996, p.11) suggest that, for the UK as a whole, 'service sector firms represent just over 70 per cent of all small firms in the economy'.[7] The 150 interviews that constituted the first year's sample were completed within the period April 1994 to May 1995. The relevant sample for our study was selected over the period 1997–8, and contained the 105 surviving firms of the initial sample.

3.3 The administered questionnaire

As has already been mentioned, the administered questionnaire was developed in the light of several years' experience in the field, coupled with extensive reading of the relevant literature surveyed elsewhere in this book. The instrument used to analyse information system development was a subset of a lengthy and detailed questionnaire covering eight main topics:

- market data;
- finance;
- costs;
- business strategy;
- management accounting system (MAS);
- human capital;
- organisation;
- technical change.

One advantage of using an administered questionnaire is that it permits the gathering of an extremely large number of data points, which can be readily coded and entered on to a computer database. Personal contact is a key factor in the success of administered questionnaires. The response rate is likely to be much higher with a personally conducted face-to-face interview than with, for example, a mailed questionnaire, which may simply be thrown away. Results should also be much more accurate, as a well-trained interviewer who understands the questionnaire is able to reply to and explain respondents' queries about meanings and exact requirements of the questions. The interviewer is able to build a rapport between himself and the respondent, and can encourage frank and honest answers as far as is possible. Thus, working together, a much more accurate response is achieved than might otherwise be the case.

---

6 Again, the Scottish Enterprise categories vary slightly in definition from those used in this study.

7 See Reid (1993, Ch.1) for detailed comparisons of the Scottish small-firms sector with that of the rest of the UK.

The data gathered on the MASs were designed to dovetail comfortably with the existing material available on the firms in question. So, in addition to this fourth year of data, there were three previous years' worth of detailed information. In essence, therefore, an unbalanced panel was developed, which contains four years' worth of annual interviews for each firm in existence, for each year of the study.[8] Much of the data gathered previously is of use to us in this current study. For example, if we wish to test the effect of contingencies on the MAS, then we need only to refer to the historical data on the database to see what happened, and when. This database already contains a great deal of detail about the strength and nature of competition in the firm's markets, about its rivals, and about technological change and its impacts, not only on the industry, but also specifically on the firms themselves. Additionally, it can provide us with data on the changing structure of the organisation and the aims and strategies developed to help deal with the growth of the firm. Importantly, we are able to pinpoint the time at which contingencies occurred, because of data held on the dates of interviews.

When considering agency theory, we are concerned with relationships within the business and, specifically, with those of principal and agent. The database stores details on the organisational hierarchy of the firm. This includes, for example, data on the extent of discretion a superior has over subordinates' workplace activities, incentive schemes such as rewarding pay structures and the extent of compliance of employees, as well as reasons for any non-compliance. The above may be useful in an application of markets and hierarchies theory, which requires us to examine organisational form. We are also able to draw on detail of the changing management structure within the firm, and the effect that increasing complexity has on the organisation's structure and strategies.

The fourth-year interviews included the original seven sections plus the new section on the development of the MAS (see Appendix), which enquired extensively into the firm's management of business information. It started by considering who prepared accounting information, at what intensity, and of what scope (e.g. profit and loss account, balance sheet, cash flow etc.). It then proceeded to look at: the capital investment decision; methods for managing costs; information flows around the business; the use of computer software; the uses of regular accounting information (e.g. to measure performance or to set budget targets); and the evolution of information over time, including the factors that influence this evolution. It concluded by looking in detail at the complexity of accounting information, under three headings: effective planning and analysis; activation and direction of daily operations; and problem-solving and decision-making. Finally, a tailpiece, permitting qualitative responses, was inserted on the reliability of accounting information and potential difficulties in using accounting information.

8 Except for occasional omissions where businessmen were difficult to pin down.

3.4 Database construction

We have described how a rich and detailed body of quantitative data was established, complemented, where relevant, with additional qualitative data. Such evidence was intended both to inform and to suggest new analytical considerations. The administered questionnaire as a whole generated a large volume of data: there were in excess of 600 quantitative variables, and an additional 50 or so qualitative variables. Available to be investigated were 105 firms, of which we finally managed to interview 84. To store the data, the preferred software was a database management system.

Software was used to create a relational database which was downward compatible with existing evidence, as well as user-friendly, in the sense of supporting structured queries and interfacing with other software packages. The specific package chosen was *Borland Paradox for Windows, Version 5.0.* The advantage of a database like *Paradox* is that it is a 'relational' database. In other words, it recognises that there is a relationship between the tables which make up the database, and enables the user to extract the specific information he/she wants from a combination of tables.

The database was therefore divided into nine tables; the first for general information, such as the respondent's name and address, the business name, the date of interview, and the person who had conducted the interview; and eight further tables, each covering a separate section of the questionnaire. Required data are selected by the researcher from the database by means of a 'query'. Typically, the files this created were then exported to *Microsoft Excel* spreadsheet files, where they were saved for further processing. In this format, the data can be read easily by several programmes, including the econometric package *Shazam* and the *Statistical Package for the Social Sciences,* better known as *SPSS.*

So, for example, if we wanted to examine the effect of size of the organisation on the frequency of provision of key budgets, we could do this quite easily with our relational database. We simply select the variables on number of directors, managers, full- and part-time workers for the years we are interested in (1, 2, 3, 4 or a combination of these), and simultaneously draw out the data relevant to key budgets. Thus, we have extracted and are able to analyse the specific data we require to answer our questions, rather than having to sort through hundreds of variables to find the relevant information. Proof of the efficiency of using such a database exists in the fact that we were able to incorporate readily the additional section on MASs towards the end of our initial four-year study.

3.5 Case selection

Having earlier stated our intention to use case study examination alongside statistical analysis, we now justify the reasons for doing so. The use of two forms of analysis is not uncommon among researchers. For example, Miles and Huberman (1984, p.151) point out that 'qualitative researchers are using multisite, multicase designs, often with multiple methods'. Sekaran (1992, p.219) agrees that 'good researchers try to obtain data ... through multiple data-collection methods'. And Yin (1993, p.59) supports the use of case studies, which he says are useful for two important reasons:

> First, the ability to incorporate an investigation of the context directly satisfies an evaluation's need to monitor and assess both the intervention and the implementation process. Second, the case study is not limited to either qualitative or quantitative data, but can incorporate both varieties of evidence.

The main advantage to us of using illustrative case study analysis, as we do here, is that, while the administered questionnaire allows us to identify tendencies for the larger full sample, using statistical techniques, a more qualitative approach permits further probing of already observed tendencies, and generates detailed descriptive evidence. Hence, it allows us to explain how our theories impact upon individual firms' management accounting systems. It also enables us to draw on the full four-years' worth of data in developing a rounded view of the introduction and development of an MAS for an individual firm.

Having now described the theories, the fieldwork and the data, and having established the desirability of some further, more qualitative, analysis, we come now to the selection of three cases for more detailed consideration. Each was chosen for the fact that it illustrated important key attributes and could provide an interesting application of one or more of the theories with which we are concerned. Case A had achieved huge growth and change in organisational structure, which had been handled competently and with highly sophisticated technology. Case B had experienced problems and declining sales, but had managed to stabilise the business, thanks in part to the reliability of its accounting information. And Case C, in a traditional industry, had managed both to increase sales and to maintain high labour productivity through efficient monitoring and disciplinary procedures. Further detail on these cases, and their illustration of the three theories under consideration in this text, can be found in Chapter 6.

3.6 Conclusion

This chapter has introduced the data that form the basis for our empirical investigation. We have established that our sample of small firms can be used with some confidence to test hypotheses and to provide results relevant to small firms, not only throughout Scotland but also throughout the UK.

The design and handling of the administered questionnaire were described in some detail. We saw how a relational database of four-years' worth of data was developed, and how this subsequently facilitated data analysis. We also explained how the new data on the management information system were integrated with retrospective material to give a dynamic aspect to the analysis. Lastly, we referred to the need for detailed analysis relating to our three key theories, and suggested why three cases might provide useful bases for a more qualitative approach. We turn now to summary statistics generated by the MAS section of the questionnaire. These enable us to characterise average tendencies of the new small firm. Let us now concentrate on the more technical data analysis mentioned earlier, to provide statistical support for our theories, as defined in Chapter 1.

Summary Statistics

4.1 Introduction

We now present an overview of the MAS data gathered during this final year of the study, by which time the businesses were between six and nine years of age. The results given are mean or average values, and are presented here to give a general impression from a descriptive overview, rather than to support any underlying theory. More sophisticated analysis is provided in Chapters 5 and 6. Here, the emphasis is on the most salient statistical features of MASs within small firms. Diagrams are used extensively to highlight such features.

4.2 Preparing information

Most owner-managers (60 per cent) were quite heavily involved in preparing the management accounting information within their business (Figure 4.1). Only 10 per cent employed an accountant to perform this task, and another 10 per cent had a partner available to help out. Eight per cent delegated the role to a manager, and 5 per cent or less let it be done by an assistant, secretary, supervisor, clerk or director. This shows the perceived importance of having 'hands-on' up-to-date accounting information, with the owner-managers typically wishing to remain well informed about such matters and therefore compiling the relevant information themselves.

Figure 4.1: Person responsible for preparing accounting information within business

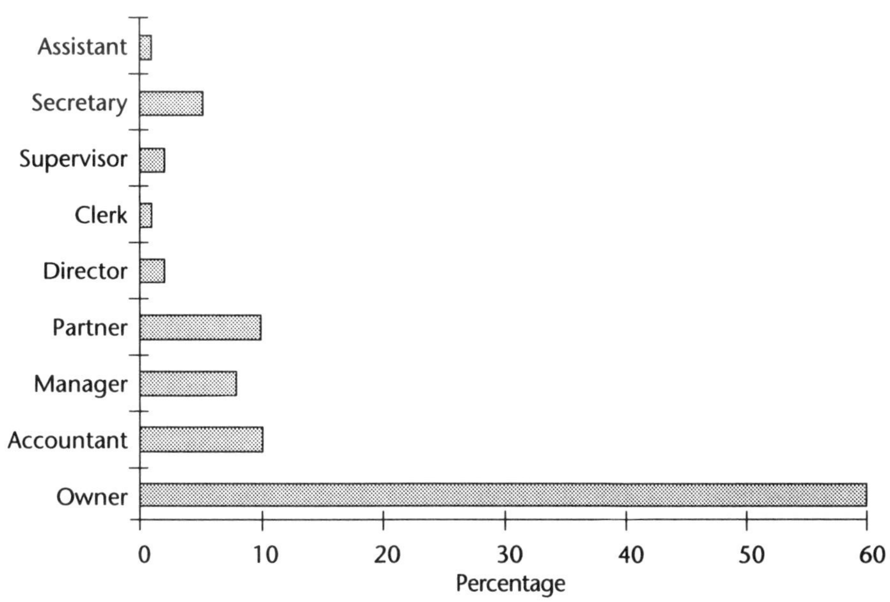

Figure 4.2: Percentage of firms that set budgets and record actual results

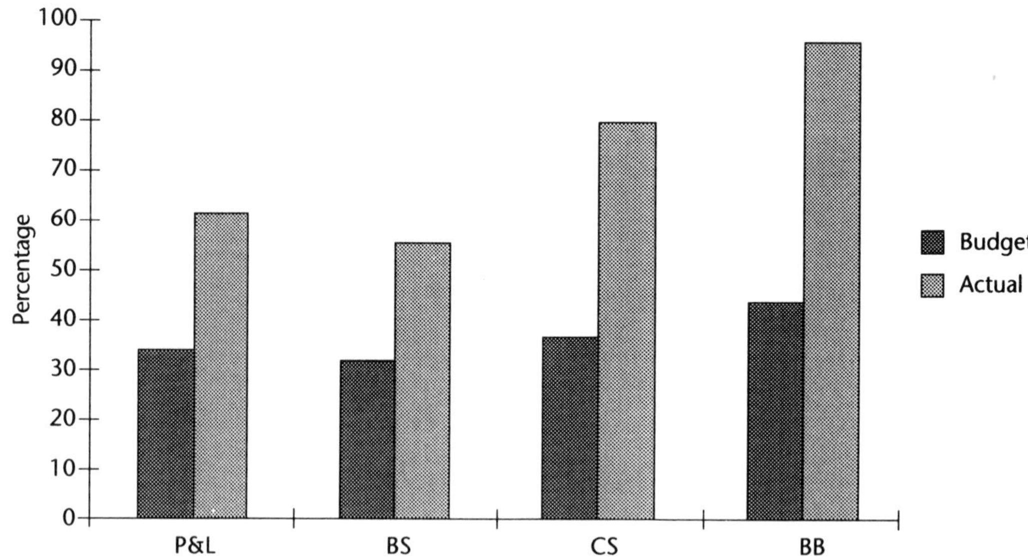

Key: P&L, profit and loss account
BS, balance sheet
CS, cash-flow statement
BB, bank balance

Up to a maximum of 42 per cent of firms interviewed said that they prepared any budgets at all (Figure 4.2). Most frequently, these related to the bank balance (42 per cent) and cash flow (36 per cent). Additionally, around 33 per cent produced budget or target profit and loss accounts and balance sheets. Actual results were recorded by a greater number of firms, with nearly all (94 per cent) having records of their bank balance, probably because these were readily supplied by their banks. Seventy-eight per cent also kept a careful note of their cash flow. Sixty-one per cent of firms produced regular profit and loss accounts, and 55 per cent produced balance sheets for use within the business. Of those which did not produce the latter statements, many were likely to be sole traders with no statutory requirement to do so, and others did not keep a record for their own use. The question was not intended to determine whether statutory financial reports were produced, but rather whether the firm had the capability of producing its own statements for internal purposes.

Of those firms that did produce financial statements, the cash flow and bank balance were the most frequently recorded, on average about once a month each (Figure 4.3). Profit and loss accounts and balance sheets were typically produced on a quarterly basis, or slightly less frequently (every 3.3 and 3.8 months, respectively). Respondents were then asked to gauge the importance of each of these statements to the managing of their firm, on a scale of 1 to 5, where 1 is low, and 5 is high importance. Of lowest importance (average 2.1) was the balance sheet, followed by the profit and loss account, which was perceived to have medium importance (average 2.5). Cash flow was quite important (average 3.61), and bank balance had the highest perceived importance, with an average of 4.24.

Figure 4.3: Frequency of measurement of key budgets, and perceived importance of each

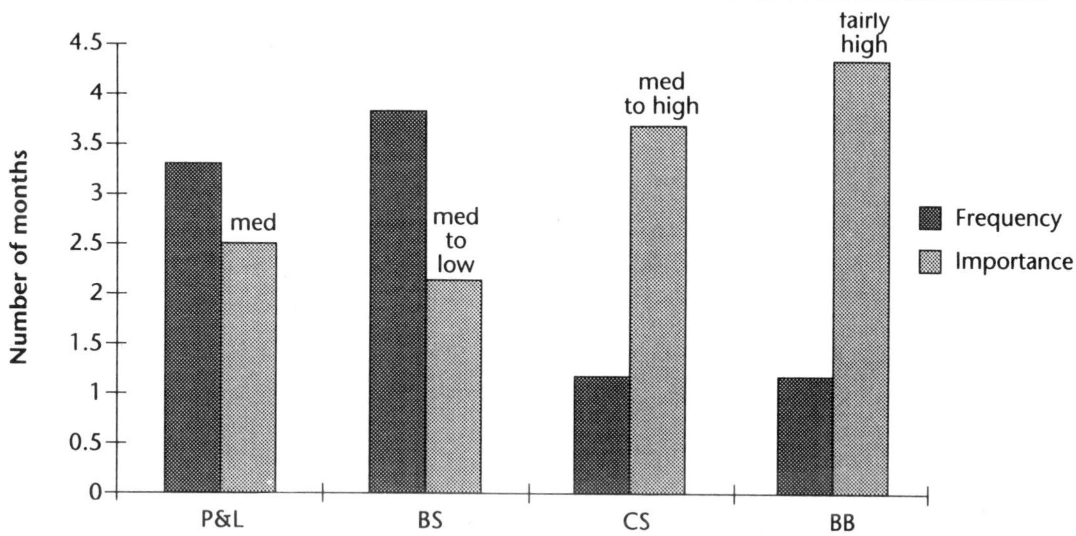

Key: P&L, profit and loss account
BS, balance sheet
CS, cash-flow statement
BB, bank balance

4.3 Capital investment

When deciding upon capital investment, many small firms will prefer to use a qualitative analysis, rather than a technical appraisal involving expected outcomes. However, 41 per cent said that they had used the payback method at some point, and a further 31 per cent claimed to have computed a measure of return on investment (Figure 4.4). The other options given to respondents were relatively unpopular, with residual income having been used by 10 per cent of firms, and net present value calculations or an internal rate of return on a project being used by only 7 per cent of businesses in each case.

When firms did use formal methods of capital investment appraisal, the earliest to be implemented was the internal rate of return on a project, usually within the first year following business inception, after an average of 7 months (Figure 4.5). Within a year and a half, residual income (15 months) and return on investment (19 months) were implemented. The payback method of assessment was typically first used a short time later, after 21 months. Where net present value was used, this was usually after about two years (28 months).

Figure 4.4: Percentage of firms that use methods of capital investment

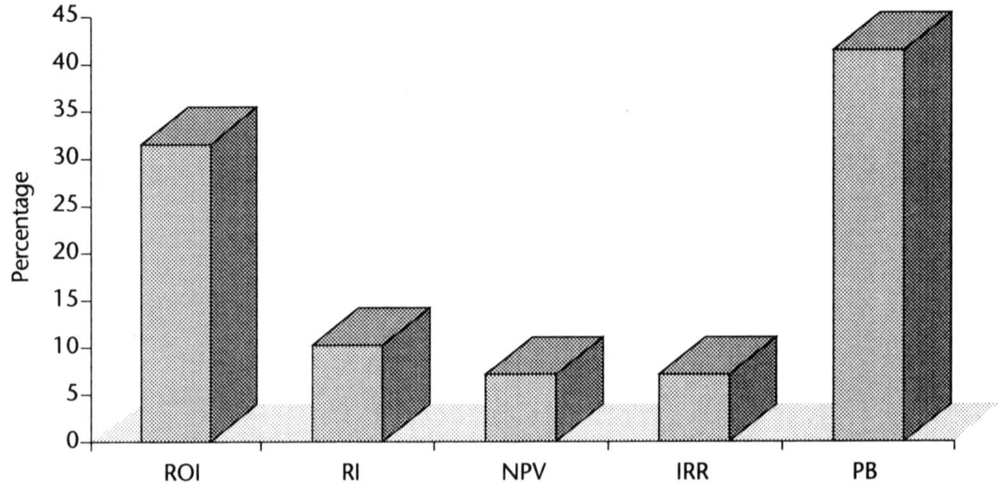

Key: ROI, return on investment
RI, residual income
NPV, net present value
IRR, internal rate of return
PB, payback period

Figure 4.5: Number of months after which methods of capital investment first implemented

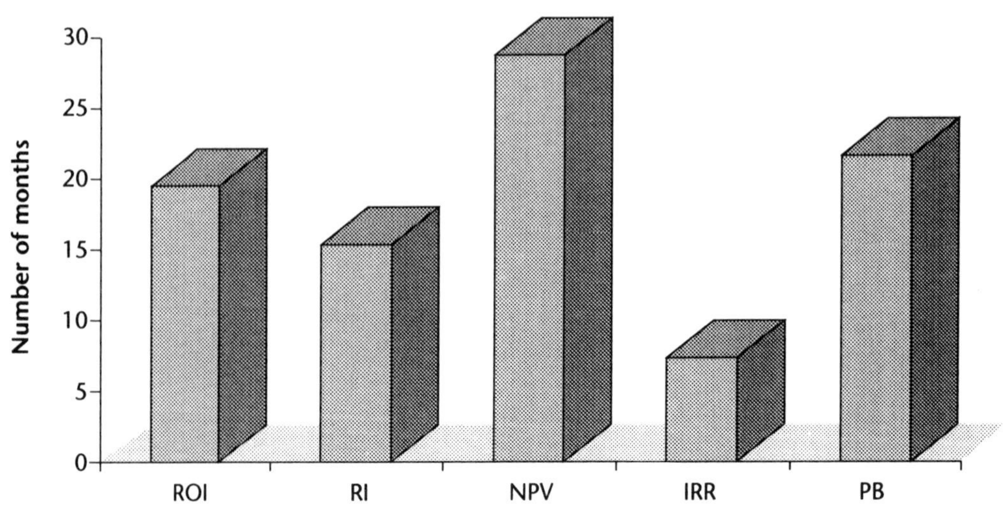

Key: ROI, return on investment
RI, residual income
NPV, net present value
IRR, internal rate of return
PB, payback period

4.4 Managing costs

Respondents were asked to divulge which methods they used for managing costs within the business. Of the options available to them, strategic pricing was seen to be the most popular, with nearly half the respondents (46 per cent) having used this (Figure 4.6), and many citing especially a preference for price discrimination. Value analysis was also widely used (43 per cent), whereby firms would identify products or activities that were not 'adding value'. Modern production practices encompassed, for example, just-in-time management and automated manufacturing, and were said to be used by 33 per cent of respondents. Twenty-five per cent claimed to have installed modern accounting practices, which might include activity-based costing or throughput accounting. Only 8 per cent found it necessary to use transfer pricing, with profit centres and pricing of individual components, and a tiny 5 per cent would utilise quantitative risk analysis in their management of costs, where this might include the calculation of expected outcomes using, for example, decision trees.

Figure 4.6: Percentage of firms using methods for managing costs

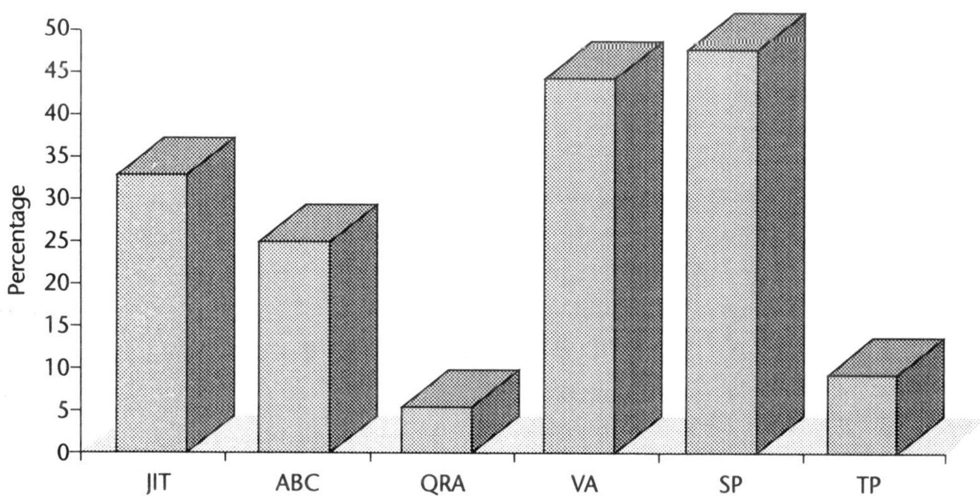

Key: JIT (just-in-time), other modern production practices
ABC, modern accounting practices, such as activity-based costing
QRA, quantitative risk analysis
VA, value analysis
SP, strategic pricing
TP, transfer pricing

Figure 4.7: Number of months after which methods for managing costs first implemented

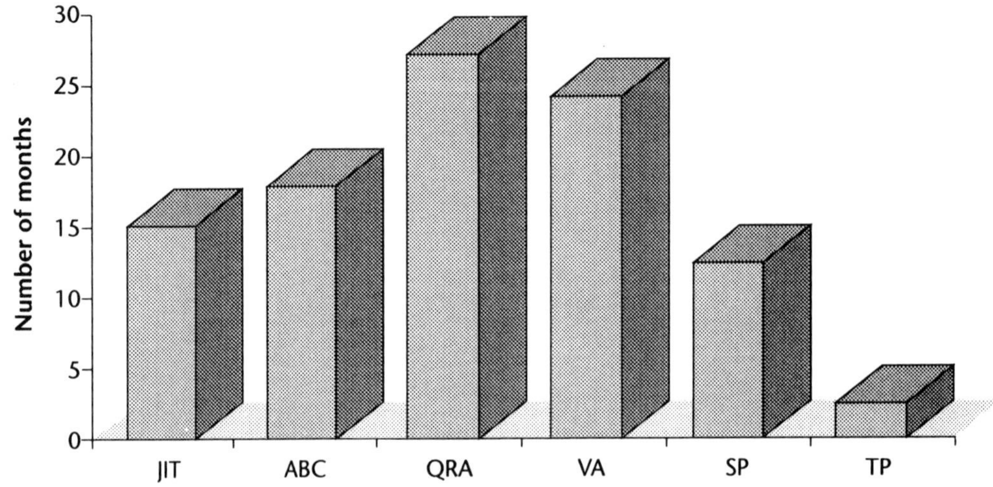

Key: JIT (just-in-time), other modern production practices
ABC, modern accounting practices, such as activity-based costing
QRA, quantitative risk analysis
VA, value analysis
SP, strategic pricing
TP, transfer pricing

On the few occasions where transfer prices were used within the business, this took place from very close to inception, during the first couple of months (Figure 4.7). Strategic pricing was something that firms latched on to fairly early on, within the first year (11 months) of trading. During the first six months of the second year in business, modern production practices such as just-in-time management (15 months), and modern accounting practices such as activity-based costing (17 months), were first used. After two years in business, value analysis first became important (23 months) and, shortly after this (26 months), those which used quantitative risk analysis first employed this method.

4.5 Information handling

Twenty-seven per cent of owner-managers thought about their business in terms of it being split up into groups or divisions, rather than simply as being a single unit (Figure 4.8). Such divisionalisation had typically occurred after two years (25 months) of trading. Entrepreneurs were then asked about the extent to which information in the business, for example on sales, profit, cash flow or work effort, was reported by segments. Fifty-nine per cent could produce information broken down by product or product group (Figure 4.9). Forty-nine per cent broke information down by customer or customer type. Twenty-six per cent provided information for departments, divisions or workgroups, and 15 per cent were interested in the breakdown of information by geographical area.

Figure 4.8: Single unit compared with divisionalised firms

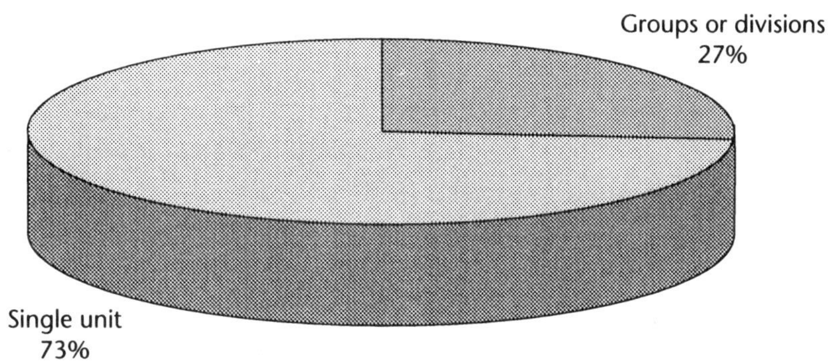

Figure 4.9: Percentage of firms that carry out segmental reporting

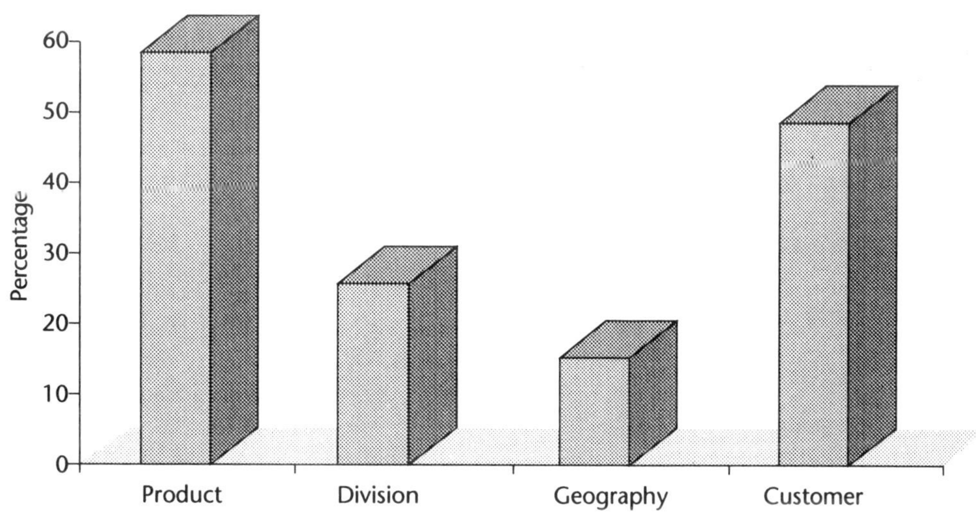

Key: Product – segmented by product or product group
Division – segmented by department or division or workgroup
Geography – segmented by geographical area
Customer – segmented by customer

Figure 4.10: Percentage of firms that use computer software compared with those that do not

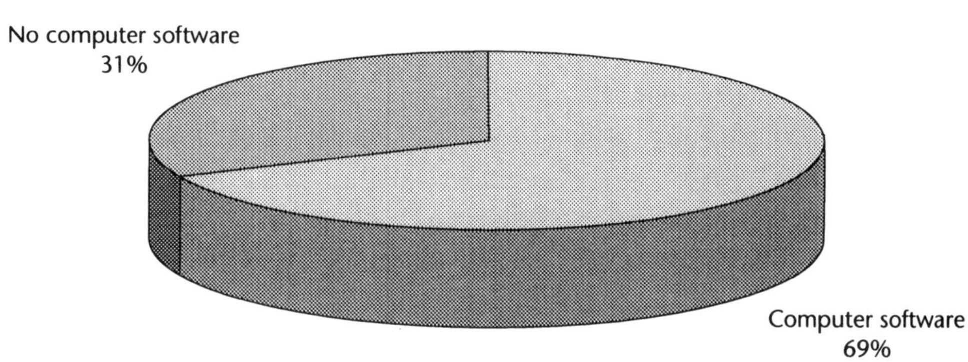

Quite a high percentage of firms (69 per cent) used computer software for handling information within the business (Figure 4.10). The vast majority of these (98 per cent) used software for storing data, whether it be financial, customer based or for stock control (Figure 4.11). Forty-four per cent of those using computer software would perform financial modelling on their PCs, and 42 per cent would carry out some kind of forecasting or simulation. Fewer would perform sensitivity analyses (26 per cent) or quantitative project appraisal using net present value or internal rates of return (25 per cent).

Figure 4.11: Aspects of information handling performed by computer software

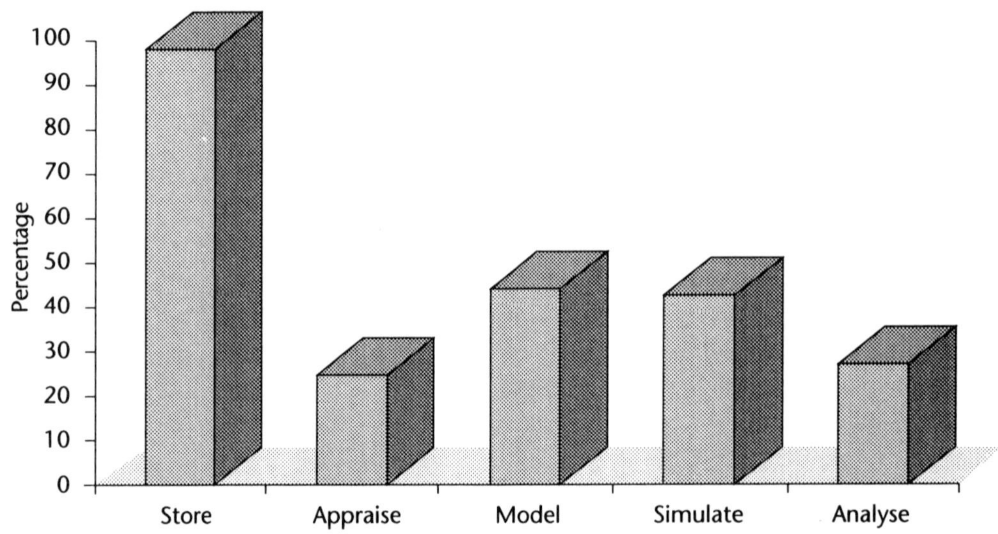

Key: Store – storing data
Appraise – project appraisal, e.g. net present value, internal rate of return
Model – financial modelling
Simulate – forecasting and simulation
Analyse – sensitivity analysis

Computers had not typically been in place from inception of the business. They were first used for storing data after 16 months (Figure 4.12). Software was then used for more technical aspects of information handling between a year and a half and two years after start-up. So forecasting and simulation were first attempted after 18 months, project appraisal after 21 months, financial modelling after 24 months, and sensitivity analysis a short time later, after 26 months.

The majority of firms (76 per cent) provided management with regular accounting information that measured the firm's performance (Figure 4.13). A further 37 per cent were provided with details of the financial implications of specific decisions and 35 per cent were supplied with information that contained budget targets. Most (72 per cent) said that this information had changed or developed over time (Figure 4.14).

Figure 4.12: Number of months after which aspects of information handling first performed by computer software

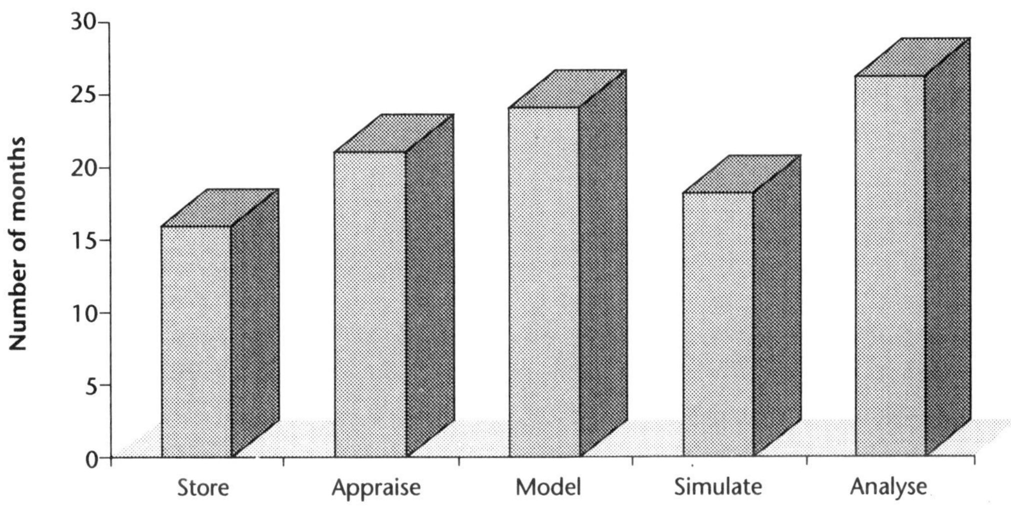

Key: Store – storing data
Appraise – project appraisal, e.g. net present value, internal rate of return
Model – financial modelling
Simulate – forecasting and simulation
Analyse – sensitivity analysis

Figure 4.13: Items on which management is provided with regular accounting information

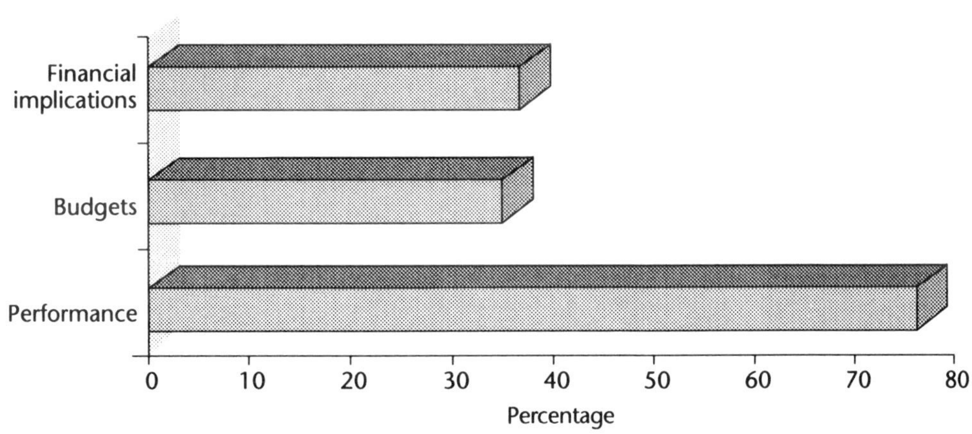

Key: Financial implications – the financial implications of specific decisions
Budgets – information containing budget targets
Performance – information that measures performance

Figure 4.14: Percentage of firms for which information has developed over time

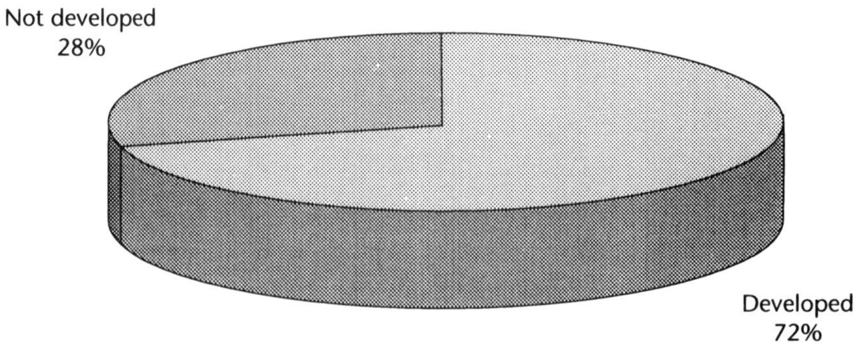

Of those owner-managers who thought that the style of information provision within their business had changed over time, several factors were thought to have prompted such developments (Figure 4.15). A growth in sales, first and foremost, was thought to have influenced change by 76 per cent of respondents. Forty-nine per cent thought that this had come about because of problems in performance. Forty-three per cent attributed change to a growth in product lines, and a further 37 per cent to growth in the number of employees in the firm. Thirty-five per cent put it down to an increase in the complexity of operations, and 33 per cent to a change in organisational structure. Fewer (14 per cent) said that change in the provision of information within the firm was due to the additional introduction of either equity or loan capital.

Figure 4.15: Factors influencing the introduction or development of management accounting information

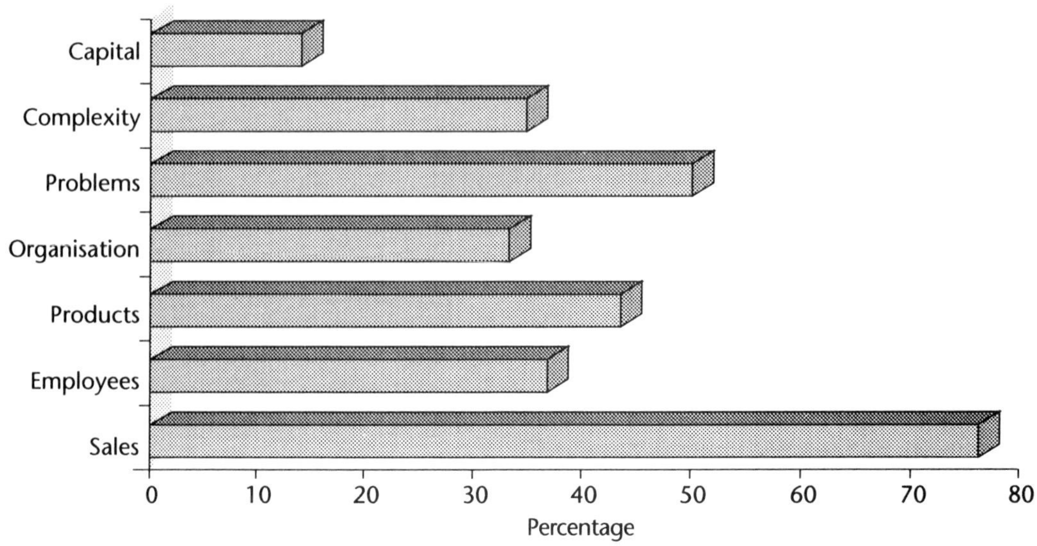

Key: Capital – introduction of new capital (equity or loan)
Complexity – increasing complexity in the operational process
Problems – experiencing problems in performance
Organisation – change in organisational structure
Products – growth in product lines
Employees – growth in number of employees
Sales – growth in sales

4.6 Complexity of information

Respondents were asked how complex was their use of accounting information, under the headings of 'Effective planning and analysis', 'Activation and direction of daily operations', and 'Problem-solving and decision-making'. Taking each category in turn, planning and analysis (Figure 4.16) was primarily assisted by the entrepreneur's use of accounting information to keep within set budgets by 54 per cent of respondents. It also helped 54 per cent to identify cost-cutting opportunities.

Forty-eight per cent thought that it helped to justify proposed expenditures. Forty-two per cent said that accounting information could help them analyse business performance against target or projected values, 41 per cent that it helped them to reach specified levels of profit, and 40 per cent to identify growth opportunities. Thirty-five per cent thought that it aided them in spotting opportunities for raising productivity. Motivation of employees was perceived to be enhanced by 27 per cent of respondents, in that they could be set targets based on the information available. However, only 18 per cent said that the performance of individual employees was measured using such information, and even fewer (16 per cent) measured the performance of teams of employees in this manner. Lastly, only 16 per cent thought that accounting information was able to assist them in identifying possibilities for improving product design.

Figure 4.16: Aspects of planning/analysis for which accounting information is used

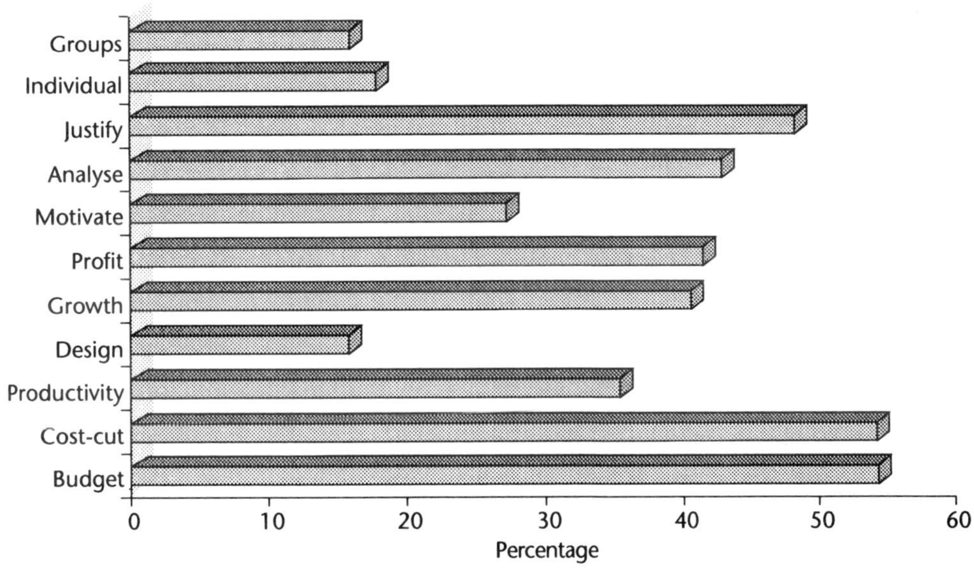

Key: Groups – measuring performance of teams of employees
Individual – measuring performance of individual employees
Justify – justifying proposed expenditures
Analyse – analysing business performance against projected or target values
Motivate – motivating employees by setting targets
Profit – reaching specified levels of profit
Growth – identifying growth opportunities
Design – identifying possibilities for improving product design
Productivity – identifying productivity-raising opportunities
Cost-cut – identifying cost-cutting opportunities
Budget – keeping within budget

In terms of activating or directing daily operations (Figure 4.17), the most important use of accounting information was that it could help the owner-manager to identify trends (47 per cent). Forty-three per cent thought it was useful for assisting in assessing and managing stock levels, or for identifying operations that had become inefficient. Forty per cent used information to measure the use of work time, and 29 per cent to measure the speed of production. When it came to quality and customer perceptions, accounting information was thought to be useful in: identifying operations that had become inefficient (38 per cent); measuring customer service and satisfaction (37 per cent); evaluating product performance (34 per cent); and ensuring that products conformed to quality standards (25 per cent). Thirty-one per cent would use information to calculate the effects of marginal changes in costs and revenues.

Figure 4.17: Aspects of activation and direction of daily operations for which accounting information is used

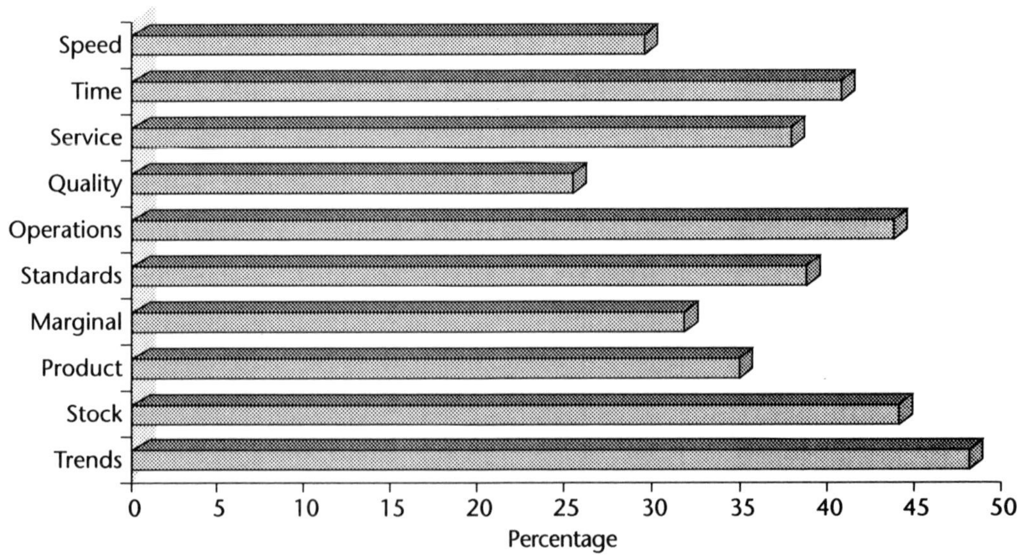

Key: Speed – measuring speed of production
Time – measuring use of work time
Service – measuring customer service/satisfaction
Quality – ensuring products conform to quality standards
Operations – identifying operations which have become inefficient
Standards – identifying standards within the firm which need revision
Marginal – calculating the effects of marginal changes in costs and revenue
Product – evaluating product performance
Stock – assessing and managing stock levels
Trends – identifying trends

When it came to problem-solving and decision-making, 61 per cent of respondents found accounting information to be useful in helping them to set prices (Figure 4.18). Forty-nine per cent used it to evaluate or choose between alternative actions or to assess a new project or investment. Forty-five per cent said it helped in determining remuneration for staff. Forty-two per cent used accounting information to analyse the riskiness of a new idea, 40 per cent to help them decide whether or not to replace old assets with new assets, and thirty-nine per cent to determine the number of products they wished to offer. Thirty-one per cent said it helped them to decide whether or not to shut down the whole or a part of the business, or to determine output levels (29 per cent). Twenty-five per cent used this information to determine the balance between what should be produced in-house and what should be contracted out. Twenty-one per cent used it to decide whether to sell off assets or part of the business, or to determine a schedule of production (19 per cent). And only 13 per cent said that accounting information would help them to assess staff for promotion or demotion.

Figure 4.18: Aspects of problem-solving and decision-making for which accounting information is used

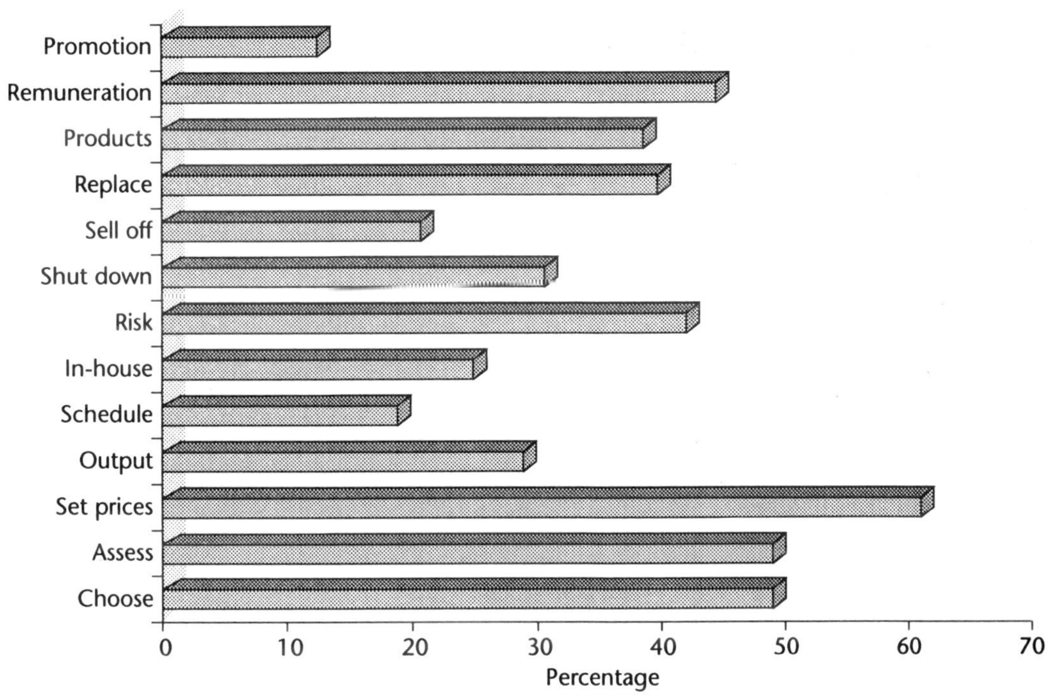

Key: Promotion – assessing staff for promotion/demotion
Remuneration – determining remuneration of staff
Products – determining number of products
Replace – deciding whether to replace old assets with new assets
Sell off – deciding whether to sell off assets or part of the business
Shut down – deciding whether or not to shut down whole or part of the business
Risk – analysing the riskiness of a new idea
In-house – determining balance between in-house production and subcontracting
Schedule – determining schedule of production
Output – determining output levels
Set prices – setting prices
Assess – assessing a new project or investment
Choose – evaluating or choosing between alternative actions

4.7 Reliability of information

There was generally a high level of confidence in the reliability of accounting information produced for use within the firm, with 96 per cent claiming it to be totally reliable (Figure 4.19). Much of this confidence came from a high level of trust: 'I trust the person who makes it,' 'She's qualified and knows the business,' and 'My husband does it,' were common explanations. Others, however, preferred to keep a close eye on the finances themselves, and so relied on their own ability to produce accurate records, saying, for example, 'I'm in control and there are double checks built in on the PC,' 'It's a very small business – I can keep my finger on the pulse,' and 'I do it myself, and it's very simple; training has helped, and I was brought up in a business environment.' Some businesses had taken further steps to ensure the reliability of their accounting information, even employing outsiders to advise or install new systems. For example, one said that 'We spent a lot of time making sure the data were 100 per cent, verifying figures with outside consultants checking;' another said that 'the system's been devised with an Enterprise Trust Director, and I see it working'. But essentially, most recognised that, to get good information out of a system, you have to put good information in to start with, saying, for example, 'We have very tight control over what goes into the book,' 'Everything is kept up to date;' and 'The information I'm looking for is factual material, as put into the PC – it's a complete record of costs, materials, labour, and so on.'

Figure 4.19: Percentage of owner-managers who thought the management accounting information produced for them to be reliable

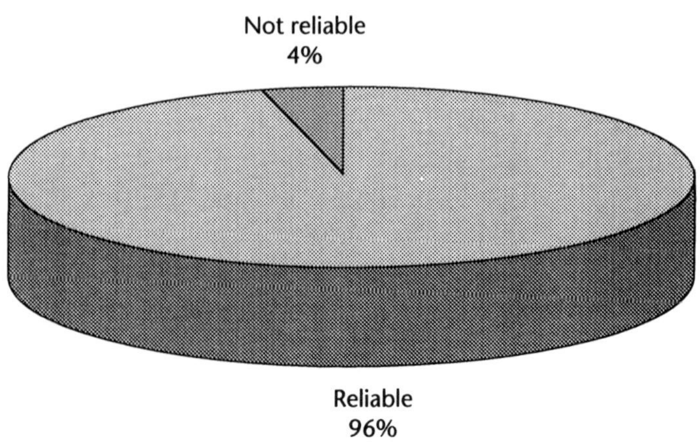

Of those owner-managers who thought that their accounting information might not be totally reliable, reasons given for this being the case included: 'It's all gobbledegook to me – if I've not got it I don't spend it; if I need it, I find the money before I get it; I have trouble getting my accountant to explain it to me without charging;' and a 'lack of knowledge, training and software' were also noted problems. However, one thought that the information was adequate for the firm's own purposes, as 'our main objective is to get the work out and the money in'.

4.8 Using information

Finally, respondents were asked whether or not they had any difficulty in using accounting information. A substantial proportion (37 per cent) said that 'yes', they did have some problems in dealing with such matters (Figure 4.20). Usually, the reasons given for their being uncomfortable with accounting information were based on a general lack of training in the area, and unfamiliarity with the potential advantages and uses of this information. For example, common responses were, 'I'm not an accountant' or 'It's not my scene.' There were also those who found the language of accountancy to be a barrier to comprehension, saying, for example, 'Fixed assets and depreciation – I can't understand what it is,' 'I know what I'm looking for, but terminology can be an alien concept to me,' or 'It depends on how technical it gets.' Some would ask their accountant to try to explain what the accounts meant, because, for example, 'I find detail difficult – I have no problem on cash flow, but I would like to improve on balance sheets' or they had problems in 'relating sales to growth in financial projections'. And an important additional reason for the owner-manager's inability to use effectively accounting information was a lack of time available to concentrate on learning how this could be done: 'We don't spend enough time to go through it and understand it,' 'There are courses, but we have no time.'

Figure 4.20: Percentage of owner-managers who had difficulty in using accounting information

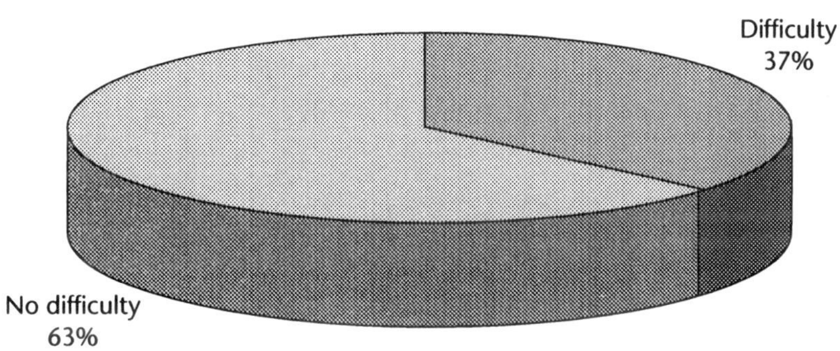

However, there were also those who said that they had no trouble in using accounting information within their firm. First of all, there were those whose information was so basic that comprehension was not an issue: 'It's not complicated, it's money in and money out; what's left is mine to spend;' 'It's pretty straightforward, simple sort of stuff that we are using.' Experience had also helped a great deal, as some explained: 'I have gained experience over the years;' and one had developed his skills through 'experience, and the fact that it's my business and I'm doing it all the time'. Training too had proved to be useful: 'Enterprise Trust courses helped;' 'I did college courses;' and 'I'm catering trained ... you have to learn how to cost a meal, how it's cost-effective, the cost of delivery, cooking, gas used, and so on.' Many were now much more proactive in seeking help from a qualified accountant: 'He explains so we understand;' 'I question him until I understand it.' And many of these firms obtained the minimum information necessary to enable them to function on the level they were at: 'I think I can get the information I need from the figures;' 'I have knowledge to a level that allows me to work;' and 'It's laid out so we can understand it.'

4.9 Conclusion

The purpose of this chapter has been to give a statistical bird's-eye view of the MAS data used in more complex contexts elsewhere in this work. It was found that the owner-manager of the small firm was still the most important person involved in preparing accounting information within the firm. Capital investment decisions tended to emphasise the payback period or return on investment, rather than discounting methods. Information handling was generally modern, with computer software being extensively used, quite often for financial modelling or sensitivity analysis, as well as for more routine data-storage tasks. Over three-quarters of the small firms provided management with regular accounting information for performance evaluation. These needs had developed significantly over time, usually in response to sales growth or performance problems. The use of accounting information was generally complex and MASs were thought to be reliable, though not always easy to use.

5

Statistical Analysis

5.1 Introduction

A considerable body of statistical evidence has already been presented in Chapters 3 and 4, but its purpose has been largely descriptive or taxonomic. While this form of evidence is important, and will not be neglected here, there is a call for more refinement in the statistical approach in order to garner the full fruits of the evidence. The structure of this chapter is as follows. First, an overview of the evidence is provided. This draws on one important theme of the existing literature on the influence of information in small firms, by emphasising performance differences across firms. Second, the contingency theory approach is explored on the data, both taxonomically (using cluster analysis) and inferentially (using regression analysis). Third, the agency approach is tested, using probit analysis. Fourth, the market and hierarchies approach is tested, using regression analysis. The chapter ends by concluding that the contingency approach is not a rival approach to the agency or market and hierarchies approaches, but may rather be regarded as incorporating, and supporting, elements of both.

5.2 Small-firm performance: an overview

One way of generating evidence to assess the value of management accounting to the small firm is to look for differences in the management accounting practices of high- and low-performing firms. The aim of this section is to provide a general statistical feel for performance differences among small firms in the sample, without appeal to advanced methods. The basic approach used is to compare the average attributes of the highest and lowest performing firms. The variable used for splitting the sample by performance was labour productivity (i.e. *Sales ÷ Headcount*).[1] The top 20 and bottom 20 firms by performance were selected, with the cut-off points being a labour productivity of no more than £15,300 for the low performers, and of at least £54,000 for the high performers. The narrative of this section is largely based on direct comparison of mean values, although in key cases (to be noted) a few salient measures of statistical inference will be introduced. In terms of basic features of the two groups of firms, it was evident that the lower performers had smaller core employment and were much more dependent on part-timers and, to some extent, trainees. Low performers had

---

1 This measure seems to provide a good sample split by performance, and relates well to other measures. Thus, the net profits of low performers were much less than those of high performers (£7k < £52k), and they also injected much less cash into the business at launch (£11k < £31k), arguably an indicator of the lesser quality of the low-performing firms.

much lower turnovers (£122k compared with £923k) and markedly smaller labour productivities (£10k compared with £127k).

In terms of their use of accounting information, there was some evidence that low performers engaged in less planning and analysis. They were also less zealous in activation and direction of their daily operations, and less energetic in problem-solving and decision-making. Using an index of overall complexity of the MAS, the low performers displayed lesser complexity than the higher performers.[2] Among low performers, it was much more likely that the owner-manager would prepare accounting information than among high performers. There was no use at all of accountants for this purpose by low performers, whereas over 20 per cent of high performers employed an accountant within the business. There is slight evidence that low performers had better internal resources for accounting than high performers, but only in the sense that, were the owner-manager to be the principal preparer of accounting information, he/she would be better qualified, on average, than in the high-performing group. Low performers were found to be prepared to use secretaries for accounting tasks (11 per cent), whereas this was unknown with high performers.

Concerning the preparation of accounting information within the firm, there was little difference in the owner-manager's involvement, as far as experience goes. The low performers spent slightly less time (16 < 20 per cent) on preparing accounting information. In general, the low performers were less attuned to the use of variance analysis. They were less likely to set targets (e.g. in terms of profit and loss, cash flow), or to record actual amounts, and made less frequent measurement (i.e. prepared accounts less frequently). The low performers also perceived techniques such as variance analysis to be less important than did high performers. An issue of interest was how information flowed through the business, as this is highly relevant to a contingency approach. It was found that low performers were less likely than high performers to split up or segment their information. The principal difference between the two categories of firms was that low performers were much less likely to segment information by customers than were high performers (37 per cent compared with 68 per cent). Both categories of firms were similar in their use of spreadsheets or computer software for handling information within their businesses. This was true for a variety of purposes to which the information could be put (e.g. data storage, financial analysis).

Low performers were less likely than high performers to provide information for the purpose of measuring performance. They were also less likely to provide management either with budget targets, or with information which displayed the financial implications of decisions. There was a slightly lesser tendency for information to have developed over time, for the low performers compared with the high performers. High performers were more able to identify the factors which had influenced the introduction or development of accounting information, and especially emphasised the importance of growth in sales and growth in product lines for such information

2 This index will be referred to again below. It is a count variable, identifying all uses of accounting information under the headings of planning, activation and decision-making.

development. The main exception to this was the relatively great emphasis given by low performers to developing accounting information when new capital was introduced into the business. Table 5.1 summarises the main findings of this initial analysis.

Table 5.1: Summary of key management accounting differences between high-performing and low-performing small firms

Characteristic	Distinguishing features of high performers' practice
General sophistication and complexity of management accounting	Higher than low performers
Production of management accounting	More likely to rely on expert help in contrast to low performers, where owner-manager with non-expert help (e.g. secretary) is more common
Time devoted to information production	More time devoted to this task
Budgeting	More likely to set targets and monitor variances
Segmentation of performance (e.g. by product or customer)	More likely to segment, particularly in respect of customer information
Performance measurement	More highly developed
Decision analysis	More likely to undertake a financial analysis of decisions
Development of management accounting	Greater propensity to develop management accounting, particularly in response to growth

We now turn from an overview of the data, in terms of sample splits by performance, to a detailed analysis of hypotheses relating to the contingency, agency, and markets and hierarchies approaches, respectively.

5.3 The contingency approach

The structure of this section is as follows. First, the idea of firm types, recognised by some contingency theorists, is given empirical content by the use of cluster analysis. Second, firm structure is explained by contingency variables such as strategy, markets and production systems. Third, the form of the AIS is explained by sub-unit interdependence, market dynamics and work-method specification, as suggested by the work of Hayes (1977).

The work of Gordon and Miller (1976) suggested that the nature of a firm's AIS would be determined by environmental and organisational factors, and by the way decisions were made (see Chapter 1). They argued that these contingent variables 'clustered' in a way which suggested a morphology of three firm types – adaptive, 'running blind' and stagnant. In this section the notion of a cluster has been taken a step further from the informal use of it by Gordon and Miller. Specifically, a statistical cluster analysis was undertaken to try to identify these, or similar, firm types, using an objective method. The hope is that this method, by grouping available evidence into a reasonably small number of classes, categories or clusters, thereby facilitates a reduction of data. This may then be suggestive of further forms of data analysis and may help to identify theoretical structures underlying the data.

Clustering was undertaken using SPSS, and the Euclidean measure of distance was adopted.[3] The aim of the technique is to group together in clusters those observation points which are most similar, and to separate out, as distinctively as possible, the clusters themselves. The variables employed in the cluster analysis were measures of: (a) the growth in sales *(SalesGro);* the change in market share *(MktChng);* the discretionary time available for decision-making as opposed to production *(Decis);* and the extent of reliance on formal, written business planning *(FormWrit).* In terms of the framework considered in the previous paragraph, the measures adopted examine dynamics, flexibility, decision-making, and formality, respectively.

It was found that the statistical cluster analysis provided a good separation of the data into three small-firm types. Their statistical attributes are summarised qualitatively in Table 5.2, where here, for expositional convenience, more generic terminology is used to describe the specific variables employed.[4] Statistically speaking, type 1 firms were separated by some distance from types 2 and 3 firms, but the latter types, while separated, were closer. These data were available for just 48 of the firms. They may be interpreted as identifying successful (type 3), less successful (type 2) and struggling (type 1) firms. However, this interpretation should be used with caution.

Table 5.2: Statistical cluster analysis

	Type 1	Type 2	Type 3
Dynamics	Low	Moderate	High
Flexibility	Poor	Moderate	High
Decision-making	Active	Moderate	Active
Formality	Low	Low	Moderate

The type 3 firms correspond in some measure to Gordon and Miller's (1976) 'adaptive firm', but the categories are by no means identical. The type 3 firm may be characterised as follows. It enjoys a high growth rate, and a high degree of penetration in terms of market share. Thus, it is properly characterised as being adaptive to a

3 Here, distance is measured, as suggested by Pythagoras' theorem, by the sum of squared differences between points.

4 The underlying data were as follows:

	SalesGro	*MktChng*	*Decis*	*FormWrit*	*n*
Type 1 firms	142 (49)	–0.4 (3)	79 (11)	0.29 (0.18)	8
Type 2 firms	176 (71)	6 (3)	57 (15)	0.33 (0.33)	17
Type 3 firms	315 (86)	9 (11)	89 (5)	0.18 (0.12)	23

Main figures are rounded mean values, with standard errors in brackets. Mean values were stable under 5 per cent trimming.

dynamic environment. It dedicates relatively little time to production of the good or delivery of the service, and, by implication, more time to management, planning, strategy, sales etc. As regards running the business, the emphasis is on formal procedure rather than intuitive governance. The type 2 firm experiences considerably lower sales growth,[5] and less market share penetration (just +6 per cent compared with +9 per cent for type 3 firms). Thus the environment is less dynamic, although the adaptiveness remains quite high. Procedurally, it is by far the most intuitively run firm type, approximating best, in this sense, to the 'running blind' type identified by Gordon and Miller (1976). Unlike types 1 and 3 firms, it allocates much more time than they do to simply delivering goods or services to customers. In doing so, it squeezes out activities like planning, managing and developing strategies etc. This, too, confirms the resemblance of this firm type to the 'running blind' category.

Finally, there is the type 1 firm, which most resembles the 'stagnant' category of Gordon and Miller (1976). These are rather poorly performing firms. Type 1 firms have experienced only moderate sales growth (about half that of type 3 firms), though certainly enough to ensure survival. However, they have been unsuccessful at adaptation and have, on average, actually lost their market shares. They are more like type 3 firms than type 2, in that they allocate a relatively high proportion of time to planning, management etc., and are relatively (but not absolutely) more formal than intuitive in their running of the firm (but, however, distinctly less formal than type 3 firms).[6] Thus, although types 1 and 3 firms are at opposite ends of the performance spectrum, they both tend to emphasise planning, management etc. This, in turn, is likely to make increased demands on AIS use and development. For type 1 firms this situation arises from the need to tackle the problems of lack of adaptation to market dynamics, and of falling market shares. For type 3 firms, planning and management are used relatively successfully to deal with problems of adapting to the dynamics of the marketplace. Their success in so doing exacts a price in terms of consequential demands for AIS development.

We turn now to the form of the small firm, and how it is influenced by contingency variables. As Chapter 1 indicated, key contingency variables include technological uncertainty, production system complexity, business strategy, market environment, and so on. Our approach to hypothesis testing has been to suggest that the scale of the firm is a key feature of its organisational form. A new measure of firm size was developed, starting from the headcount, by weighting full-time workers at 100 per cent, part-time workers at 50 per cent, and trainees at 25 per cent. Thus, worker types play a role in this organisational measure, and their relative significance within the small firm is captured by a weighting scheme. This organisational variable will be described as the weighted headcount measure *(HeadCnt)*. Four classes of

---

5 About 176 per cent over four years, compared with 315 per cent over four years for type 3 firms.

6 However, all firms were more towards the intuitive end of the spectrum, so this statement is only concerned with relative differences.

contingency variables were identified to explain this organisational measure: technological uncertainty; production systems; strategy; and markets. There were several variables in each class, as indicated in Table 5.3. In this table, regression coefficients (and corresponding *t*-values, indicating statistical significance) are given in columns 3 and 4. In all, twelve variables (and a constant term) are used to explain the weighted headcount measure of organisational form (namely the dependent variable, *HeadCnt).*

Table 5.3: Four classes of contingency variables

Contingencies	Variables	Coefficients	*t*-values
Technological uncertainty	*ProcPres*	–0.617	–0.298
	ProdPres	2.934	1.404
	TechChng	–2.473	–0.960
Production systems	*Attribut*	1.537	1.811*
	Wages	$5.932.10^{-2}$	1.146
	CostCut	0.513	0.193
Strategy	*Impact*	0.177	2.926†
	SacStak	1.007	0.423
	SmlProf	–0.411	0.128
Market	*MktShr1*	$7.645.10^{-2}$	1.603
	MajRiv	0.152	2.416†
	CompAll	1.954	1.258
	Constant	–11.359	–1.836

Notes: Adjusted $R^2 = 0.295$; $F = 3.369$†
* Statistically significant; † Highly statistically significant

For cross-section models of this sort, the adjusted R^2 is high (at approximately 0.3)[7] and the *F* statistic for the regression as a whole is highly statistically significant (prob. level = 0.001).[8] The groupings of variables under the four contingencies listed are as follows. Under 'Technological uncertainty' the variables are: *ProcPres,* which measures the competitive pressure put on a small firm by its rivals' process innovations; *ProdPres,* which measures the same effect, but with regard to product innovations;[9] and *TechChng,* which measures the extent of technical change in the industry. None of these variables is significant. There is just the slightest hint that the competitive pressure of product innovation encourages larger size, in a weighted headcount sense, but this has low significance (prob. level = 0.166).

---

7 In the discussion that follows, the coefficient of multiple determination (R2) will be prefaced with the word 'adjusted' if an adjustment for degrees of freedom has been made.

8 This tests the so-called 'null hypothesis', that all the coefficients in the regression are zero (i.e. that the regression relationship as a whole is insignificant). This hypothesis is clearly rejected in this case.

9 A process innovation involves doing an existing production activity in a new and more efficient way. A product innovation involves producing an entirely new good to meet a new perceived demand. Both processes of innovation, and reactions to it, are fraught with uncertainty.

Turning now to 'Production systems' contingencies, there are three variables to be considered: *Attribut,* which measures the extent to which elements of cost are attributed to products; *Wages,* which measures the wage bill component in total cost; and *CostCut,* which measures whether the small firm could gain a competitive advantage by extreme cost cutting. All these variables appear to have a positive relationship with the dependent variable, but only *Attribut* has a significant relationship (prob. level = 0.075). That is, larger firms, in terms of weighted headcount, tend to take greater measures to attribute elements of costs to products (e.g. materials, labour, sales etc.).

The third category of contingency, namely 'Strategy', is measured by three variables: *Impact,* which measures how far the firm looks ahead in considering the impact of decisions; *SacStak,* which measures whether the owner-manager is willing to sacrifice a proportion of his or her stake in the firm, in order to promote its growth; and *SmlProf,* which measures whether he or she is willing to accept smaller profits for a while, in order to expand the business. The last two variables are clearly statistically insignificant in Table 5.3, but the *Impact* variable has a strong positive effect upon the dependent variable and is highly statistically significant (prob. level = 0.005). That is to say, small firms that plan ahead, looking to the future impact effects of their current decisions, are able to negotiate better the organisational change involved in becoming a higher weighted headcount firm.

Finally, the last group of contingent variables comes under the 'Market' heading. There are three of these variables, and they have the following interpretation. *MktShr1* measures the market share of the most important product group or range, according to sales. *MajRiv* measures the number of major rivals that the small firm has. *CompAll* measures how strong (overall) competition is, within the small firm's main market. Market share and overall competition have no statistically significant effect on the dependent variable. By contrast, the effect of number of major rivals is positive and highly statistically significant. Thus close competitive pressure, as measured by major rivals, seems to be a stimulus to organisational change, as measured by weighted headcount. Considering the regression as a whole in Table 5.3, it is very illuminating from a statistical and theoretical standpoint. First, it shows that an index of a certain type of organisational development *(HeadCnt)* can be well explained by contingencies. In that sense, contingency theory is vindicated. Further, under each of the major headings of contingencies, such as are widely discussed in the literature, notably technological uncertainty, production systems, business strategy and market environment, some variables appear to have measurable and significant effects on organisational change, as measured by weighted headcount. Specifically, the competitive pressure of product innovation, complex costing systems, far-sighted decision-making, and competitive pressure from major rivals, all seem to be vectors of change in organisational form.[10]

10 These effects are highly significant for the last three contingency variables mentioned, but less so for the first (for which the prob. level is 17 per cent).

Table 5.4: Three classes of contingency variables

Contingencies	Variables	Coefficients	*t*-statistics
Production systems	*Attribut*	1.297	1.825*
Strategy	*Impact*	0.180	3.297†
Market	*MktShr1*	$7.811.10^{-2}$	1.980*
	MajRiv	0.160	3.046†
	CompAll	2.520	2.009†
	Constant	–10.161	–2.267†

Notes: Adjusted $R^2 = 0.325$; $F = 8.213$†
* Statistically significant; † Highly statistically significant

The statistical picture can be further sharpened by considering a more parsimonious regression, as reported in Table 5.4. The effect of dropping the insignificant variables of Table 5.3 is fairly dramatic. The adjusted R^2 is higher, as is the F statistic (prob. level < 0.001), which measures the overall significance of the regression relationship. All the contingency variables in Table 5.4 now have strong positive effects on the dependent variable. This is partly because some of the more 'noisy' variables, which contribute little to the explanation of the dependent variable in the first regressions (Table 5.3), are now absent.

Table 5.4 now says something very clearly about contingency theory as applied to small firms. The role of technological uncertainty now appears to be relatively unimportant. This has been seen as a key contingency in the literature, and indeed can be traced back to the very earliest works on the subject, e.g. Burns and Stalker (1961). However, the evidence in that early work was based on a very large enterprise, characterised by high technological intensity.[11] By contrast, most small firms, particularly most micro-firms, do not have high technological intensity. The main innovative step is the launch of the business itself. But typically micro-firms do not engage in serious R&D. They are more likely to protect small innovative steps by keeping ahead of their rivals than by recourse to formal methods of protecting intellectual property, like patents and trademarks.

On the other hand, the production systems and strategy components of contingency do have, at least, some effects coming through strongly. The use of a detailed costing system appears important (*Attribut,* prob. level = 0.072), as does a long-run view of decision-making (*Impact,* prob. level = 0.002). However, the major effect of contingency variables for small firms, especially those at the smaller end of the scale, seems to derive from the market environment. All three contingency variables for this category are statistically significant (and two of them highly so): *MktShr1,* market share (prob. level = 0.052); *MajRiv,* major rivals (prob. level = 0.003);

11 See, for example, the works by Reid et al. (1996) and by Reid and Roberts (1996) which examine the UK scientific instrument industry over a ten-year period. There, technological intensity, as measured by patent count divided by percentage of gross domestic product (GDP) attributable to this industry, is one of the highest in any UK industrial sector.

and *CompAll,* overall competition (prob. level = 0.048). In short, rivalry and competition appear to be the major contingencies which modify organisational form for the small firm. This is not to reject the contingency hypothesis, but to modify its form to take account of the special attributes which small firms display.

We turn next to a further aspect of contingency analysis, bearing in mind that we have now left the general framework largely intact. This aspect emphasises the predictive implications of contingency. In particular, Hayes (1977) has proposed within this framework that MAS practices differ largely because of three contingent variables: sub-unit interdependence; market dynamics; and work methods. Recent work by Libby and Waterhouse (1996) follows on from this approach by trying to explain MAS development by factors like decentralisation, competition and organisation practice (see Chapter 2). Here, we follow and extend this literature.

Our starting point is a measure of MAS complexity. An aggregate way of looking at the MAS is to measure its complexity *(Complex)* as a count variable, covering all uses of accounting information under the general headings of planning, activation and decision-making. A statistical model was created which grouped together four measures of sub-unit interdependence, three measures of market dynamics and three measures of workplace methods. Thus sub-unit interdependence was looked at in terms of whether the information flow within the business was divided up in any way *(Divide)* (e.g. by customers or by geographic areas). Market dynamics were looked at in terms of variables like change in market share *(MktChng),* extent of market *(Market)* (e.g. local, regional, national, international) and growth of sales *(SalesGro).* The specification of work methods was looked at in terms of variables like *Discret,* the amount of discretion a superior has over a subordinate; *Author,* the flexibility for exercise of authority at any lower level; and *StdProc1,* the extent to which monitoring is standard or discretionary. Table 5.5 reports on a regression which uses MAS complexity as the dependent variable *(Complex)* and six regressors, grouped under the headings: sub-unit interdependence; market dynamics; and work methods.

Table 5.5: MAS complexity as a dependent variable

Category	Variable	Coefficient	*t*-value
Sub-unit interdependence	*Define*	0.437	0.195
	KnowOth	1.497	0.226
	TakeOth	5.407	1.209
	Divide	5.690	1.807*
Market dynamics	*SalesGro*	$-4.31.10^{-3}$	–0.530
	Market	0.253	0.193
	MktChng	$-4.45.10^{-2}$	–0.741
Work methods	*Discret*	4.499	2.269†
	Author	–3.247	–0.826
	StdProc1	–3.873	–0.981
	Constant	–9.776	–0.841

Notes: R^2 = 0.348; F = 1.176

* Statistically significant; † Highly statistically significant

The satisfactory estimation of this regression is hampered by the frequent presence of missing values, which means it was only estimated for 32 firms. The R^2 is satisfactory, but the adjusted R^2 is very low (0.052) and the F statistic of 1.176 is barely significant. Only two of the regressors, *Divide* (prob. level = 0.084), a 'Sub-unit interdependence' variable, and *Discret* (prob. level = 0.033), a measure of a superior's discretion over a subordinate, are statistically significant. This is not a trivial result, but does not give one as much confidence in the predictions of contingency theory as one would wish. A parsimonious regression is reported in Table 5.6.

For the regression of Table 5.6, the R^2 is 0.159, but the adjusted R^2 is again low (0.089) and the F statistic is only significant at the 8 per cent level. However, a slightly improved precision of estimation is possible if one focuses on just one category of variables, 'Sub-unit interdependence'. The *Define* variable is marginally significant, at conventional significance levels (prob. level = 0.112), and the *Divide* variable is more clearly statistically significant, as it was in the regression of Table 5.5. *Define* refers to the precision with which areas of specialisation are defined within the small firm, and *Divide* refers to the extent to which the business is conceived to be split up into groups, divisions or branches, as distinct from being conceived as a single unit.

Table 5.6: Parsimonious regression related to one category

Category	Variable	Coefficient	*t*-value
Sub-unit interdependence	*Define*	2.315	1.621*
	KnowOth	–3.287	–0.969
	TakeOth	4.470	1.370
	Divide	5.218	2.573†
	Constant	7.861	1.986*

Notes: $R^2 = 0.159$; $F = 2.270$*
* Statistically significant; † Highly statistically significant

The regression of Table 5.6 gives some support to the idea that MAS complexity is positively associated with well-defined specialisation within the small firm, and the subdivision of it into parts. Together, the regressions of Tables 5.5 and 5.6 give limited, if not powerful, support to some of the predictions of contingency theory. Considered overall, contingency theory is well supported by the triangulation of three bodies of statistical evidence: the cluster analysis, detecting three principal firm types; the regression analysis of the effects of contingencies on organisational form; and the regression analysis of the effects of sub-unit interdependence, market dynamics and workplace methods on MAS complexity. Further, the last two methods suggest that perhaps the determinants of the form of the small firm's MAS would be better viewed in alternative, but in some measure complementary, frameworks. Two such methods, to be considered in the next section, are agency analysis and markets and hierarchies analysis. As we shall see, all three methods of approach are interconnected.

5.4 Agency and markets v. hierarchies approaches[12]

Information is a crucial aspect of agency analysis because, in a principal–agent relationship, the agent may take actions which are concealed from the principal, and indeed may not be in the latter's interest. This insight extends to hierarchies, for they may be viewed as no more than tiered principal–agent relationships.[13] Management accounting may naturally be viewed from a principal–agent perspective, as first observed by Baiman (1982) and subsequently developed by researchers such as Scapens (1991), because it provides an empirical framework within which information flows can be embedded, for the purposes of monitoring, performance evaluation and control.

The difficulty with agency theory is that it is very hard to test, because everything happens at the level of the individual contract. Reid (1998) has tried to surmount this difficulty by analysing detailed primary source data on individual contracting practices. Necessarily, much analysis of this sort must be qualitative. It remains a considerable challenge to devise suitable quantitative tests of hypotheses suggested by agency analysis. A brief characterisation of each side of the agency relationship would see the principal monitoring, directing and rewarding the agent, supplying information, effort and shirking.

The interaction of these two effects should explain the existence and form of the MAS. For example, one might hypothesise that the MAS was a function of incentives, complexity and information asymmetry. Unfortunately, many of the relevant variables are unknown, or poorly defined, and crude hypotheses are not well supported. To illustrate, one might investigate the relationship between informal monitoring and incentivisation, expecting them to be inversely related. A possible proxy for informal monitoring is the frequency with which superiors review subordinates, on which we do have evidence, in the shape of the variable *Revsub*. The extent of incentivisation within the hierarchy that some small firms have can be measured by the wage gradient as you get promoted. We can measure this by the ratio which the top salary bears to the bottom salary in the small firm, using the variable *Salev1*. Unfortunately, the sample size is just 32 firms, given missing data. No correlation can be found between these variables ($R^2 = 0.004$; and $F = 0.117$, with prob. level = 0.735).

However, other approaches can be used. One can ask what determines the remuneration of personnel within the firm in terms of incentivisation, standard procedures and workplace direction. A more refined approach would be to ask what explains the usage of accounting information to evaluate the firm's employees. A choice for the dependent variable is *ProsolM*. It is a binary variable which determines whether the small firm uses accounting information to assess staff for promotion or demotion.

Table 5.7 reports on probit estimates of the influence of incentives, standard procedures and workplace task assignment.[14] The R^2 is high for models of this sort,

---

12 The agency approach is often also called the principal–agent approach.

13 See, for example, the paper by Radner (1985), who develops this theme in some detail.

14 Probit estimates were undertaken using *Shazam* (*Version 8.0*) software.

and the overall probit is highly statistically significant, judged by a likelihood ratio test. *Salev1* and *Undact* are neither of them statistically significant at conventional levels. There is the hint that a more incentivised structure (the *Salev1* variable) encourages the use of accounting information in the performance evaluation of staff (the variable *ProsolM*), and the elasticity is high. The *Undact* variable seeks to get an understanding of information asymmetry, and measures whether employees (as agents) understand and act on instructions issued by managers (as principals).

Table 5.7: Probit estimates of the influence of incentives

Variable	Coefficient	*t*-ratio	Elasticity
Salev1	0.289	1.335	0.659
StdProc	1.254	2.306*	0.490
UndAct	–0.136	–0.516	–0.347
Constant	–1.412	–1.130	–1.310

Notes: Cragg-Uhler $R^2 = 0.372$; $\chi^2 = 10.42$*
* Highly statistically significant

There is a positive, but not highly statistically significant, relationship (prob. level = 0.10) between the use of accounting data for assessing staff for promotion or demotion and the degree of incentivisation of the remuneration structure. This seems to suggest that highly incentivised structures, which tend to stimulate high performance, can only be held in place if supported by an accounting system capable of measuring employees' relative success or failure, and making rewards accordingly.

Although not statistically significant, at conventionally utilised levels, this positive result is robust across different specifications of the model. Further, the coefficient of *Salev1* has a very high elasticity, suggesting that there is a powerful need to support a strongly incentivised salary structure with a well-developed accounting information system. Also important in the probit of Table 5.7 is the positive relationship between discretionary procedures (*StdProc* = 1) and the use of accounting information for staff promotion or demotion. The elasticity here is also quite large, suggesting that the link has considerable quantitative impact, and the coefficient of *StdProc* is highly statistically significant. A measure of subordinate compliance (*UndAct* = 1) is also included in this probit, but its effect is entirely statistically insignificant.

In Table 5.7 the relevant dependent variable was one which related to effective planning and analysis (namely *ProsolM,* the use of accounting information to assess staff for promotion and demotion). A different dependent variable is used for the probit of Table 5.8 which, however, continues to use the same independent variables. Here, the dependent variable, again based on measures of the complexity of accounting information, is used, this time drawn from under the heading of problem-solving and decision-making. This dependent variable is *PlananK,* which measures the extent to which accounting information is used (*PlananK* = 1) to determine the scope of the small firm's operations, in terms of product range.

Table 5.8: Probit estimates of problem-solving and decision-making

Variable	Coefficient	t-ratio	Elasticity
Salev1	0.404	1.935*	1.013
StdProc	0.843	1.502	0.309
UndAct	0.760	0.919	2.118
Constant	–4.085	–1.581	–3.898

Notes: Cragg–Uhler R^2 = 0.346; χ^2= 9.582†
* Statistically significant; † Highly statistically significant

It is found that increasing the complexity of accounting information to increase the scope of the firm is positively associated with an incentivised salary structure. This effect is statistically significant, and has a high elasticity. Standard procedures which are discretionary (*StdProc* = 1) are also positively associated with increased complexity of accounting provision, in the sense of further scope on the product range (though the effect is not highly statistically significant (prob. level = 0.08) for the relatively small sample used). Compliance, as measured by *UndAct,* is definitely statistically insignificant. Taken together, the probits of Table 5.7 and Table 5.8 suggest that accounting complexity and incentivised staff remuneration systems tend to go hand in hand. This supports the agency approach, in that it is only possible to keep an incentive system in place, and to allow discretionary flexibility in monitoring,[15] if it is supported by a sufficiently complex accounting system, along the dimensions of effective planning and analysis, and of problem-solving and decision-making.

Finally, we turn to the markets v. hierarchies approach. It is to be noted that the above is not inconsistent with markets and hierarchies, and indeed has already appealed to much of the nomenclature of this literature, including hierarchy itself (e.g. in the definition of *Salev1,* the ratio of the salary at the top of the hierarchy pyramid to that of the bottom of the pyramid), and compliance. Recall that the generation of hierarchy within the firm is typically associated with control loss, in the absence of remedial action. As a general proposition, the growth of a small firm is associated with the creation of hierarchy. The original founder of the firm devolves tasks to managers (trained in the founder's principles) as growth proceeds. Then tasks formerly undertaken by the owner in the early days of the firm are now undertaken by the subordinates of the managers. However, information about ground operations is no longer at the owner-manager's fingertips, but filters up from the bottom of the hierarchy pyramid, with some degradation at each stage. A rational way of attenuating this, and thus to avoid performance deterioration of the firm through control loss, is to implement an information system. This would be expected to increase in complexity as the extent of hierarchy proliferated.

Referring back to Figure 1.3, we note that in the hierarchy pyramid the downward flow of planning co-ordination and control is matched by an upward flow of accountability for performance. The relationship suggested there, within a markets and hierarchies framework, was tested by multiple regression methods of the sort

15 As suggested by the *StdProc* variable.

already used extensively above. For the sake of brevity, these further results will be treated in less detail. Generally speaking, it was found that the provision of accounting information for performance (the upward flow in the hierarchy diagram) was positively associated with the provision of information for planning (the downward flow in the hierarchy diagram).

At its simplest level, a general planning variable *(Plan)* was used, this being a count variable of all planning measures. Then the flow of accounting information *(AccInfo)* was explained by this *Plan* variable in a linear regression, using 82 observations. The R^2 was 0.325 and the F statistic was 39.02, which is highly statistically significant (prob. level = 0.000). The coefficient on the *Plan* variable was positive and highly statistically significant (t = 2.46; prob. level = 0.000). This result can be generalised by using more complex measures of planning.[16]

5.5 Conclusion

Three types of theory have been tested in this chapter – contingency theory, agency theory, and markets and hierarchies theory. There is a sense in which agency theory is nested in hierarchy theory, which in turn is nested in contingency theory. Thus, refuting contingency theory lock, stock and barrel would refute both the agency and hierarchies theories. On the other hand, supporting agency and hierarchies theories would tend to support contingency theory, but would not entirely vindicate it. Finally, refuting agency theory, or hierarchy theory (or both) would refute contingency theory.[17]

The results of this chapter certainly support agency and markets and hierarchies theory. In this sense the evidence also supports contingency theory. However, contingency theory, partly because it is informally rather than mathematically expressed, is a more amorphous theory and therefore harder to test. Reflecting this, the greater weight of the statistical analysis was devoted to testing contingency theory. The results were generally supportive of contingency theory, and were not subversive of either the agency or hierarchies theories. A significant finding, as applied to the small firms (indeed, generally micro-firms) of this sample, was that technological uncertainty appeared to be relatively unimportant in explaining organisational form, though elements of production, strategy and markets (the other three main classes of contingency) were important. Though many factors were found to play a role in influencing MAS complexity, the dominant ones related to sub-unit inter-dependence.[18] Overall, the evidence points to support for the contingency theory approach, appropriately modified to the small-firms context.

---

16 If eleven distinct planning variables are used in a regression, instead of the aggregate Plan measure, with AccInfo again as the dependent variable, then we get $R^2 = 0.395$ and $F = 4.207$ (prob. level = 0.000).

17 The taxonomy would be complete by saying that refuting agency theory would refute hierarchy theory.

18 Arguably, this itself is functionally related to the organisational complexity of the small firm.

6

Case Studies

6.1 Introduction

Chapter 5 has shown how certain aspects of contingency, agency and markets v. hierarchies theories can be used as a framework for analysing the introduction and development of a management information system (MIS). The analysis used statistical techniques to establish the key determinants of such changes for a group of small firms. Now, in order to illustrate more clearly how these theories impact upon individual firms, three case studies are presented. These three firms were chosen because they all exhibited some interesting changes over the four years during which they were investigated. First, they displayed significant growth (or decline) in sales and/or employment. Second, the information systems within their businesses were both relatively sophisticated and well utilised. Third, they exhibited differences which offer insightful contrasts in the nature and development of management accounting.

Case A investigates a computer software business that experienced impressive growth in sales and employment. Although it started with a computing system that held information on all aspects of the business, organisational change led to modifications and improvements in this system. Relationships between principals and agents played a key role in the management of information within this business, which managed successfully to avoid potential problems of information asymmetry and moral hazard.

Case B considers a small cable assembly business, which had experienced problems in performance and had needed to cut back on staff. Although the business itself changed considerably over four years, its management accounting system did not, owing to the fact that it was already well developed from day one. The forward-thinking managers were able to justify the initial time and money spent on developing their accounting information and monitoring systems, as they eventually helped the business to cope with periods of difficulty, when it might otherwise have failed.

Finally, Case C examines a contract joinery firm, which experienced impressive growth in every year of the study. This business exhibits particularly interesting changes in its hierarchy and in its use of disciplinary devices. The analysis of this case shows how agency problems, such as information asymmetry, were reduced, thanks to improved monitoring, and how an increased threat of dismissal led to the attenuation of moral hazard. Thus these three cases help to clarify our hypotheses and to illustrate operational aspects of the theories in which we are interested.

6.2 Case Study A: Computer software design

The company was set up at the start of 1992 by a computer science graduate who had wanted to create a business that would write and produce all categories of multimedia software. Until the time that he was originally contacted with a request for his assistance in the study, this entrepreneur had run the business from his own home. However, in 1994 he moved into office premises on the edge of an industrial estate in Dundee. From that point, the company experienced tremendous growth, changes in its organisational and legal form, and a move to much larger premises in Dunfermline. It rapidly became one of the most successful new starts of its cohort in the UK.

Table 6.1 presents some of the key characteristics of the business over time. From having only one director and a handful of staff initially, the business grew to a total of 46 personnel. Its legal structure had been modified accordingly, from a sole tradership, through private limited company status, right up to a public company, listed on the alternative investment market (AIM), and aiming for main market listing within the next eighteen months to two years. This full listing was to take place either in the UK or, more likely, in the USA, the main outlet for the company's end product.

Table 6.1: Key characteristics

	Year 1	Year 2	Year 3	Year 4
Directors	1	1	2	2
Managers	0	1	5	6
Full-time employees	2	7	13	38
Part-time employees	1	2	1	0
Total headcount	4	11	21	46
Legal form	Sole trader	Private limited company	Private limited company	Public company
No. of products	15	13	5	2
Turnover	£150,000	£220,000	£587,000	£1,400,000
Net profit	£30,000	–(£60,000)	–(£150,000)	–(£91,000)

Having started the business with the intention of covering a wide market, and an aim to produce primarily educational software, while also dabbling in 'image retrieval' and various contract research projects, the owner-manager had gradually begun to focus solely on the provision of two main products, these both falling under the umbrella of computer games. He considered that the international market offered the best prospects for growth and that the most opportunity for a company such as his, was to produce new and original games.

The relatively high turnover of £150,000 in the first year grew year on year to an impressively high £1,400,000 for a business not yet six years old. Net profits, however, did not grow, but instead fell to losses between years 1 and 2, and years 3 and 4, rallying back by year 4 to a smaller loss of £91,000. But this had been expected: the company was in a development phase and spending years on creating a product with market-beating potential. Projected losses had not, in any case, prevented venture capitalists from investing in the business. They obviously rated its potential highly, and would not have risked their money without a detailed and thorough investigation of the firm's past performance and future potential.[1]

6.2.1 *The environment*

Over the four years during which this business was tracked, the number of major rivals, as perceived by the owner-manager, had fluctuated (Table 6.2). Initially, as the firm itself had not focused on a specific niche, but instead chose to offer as many varied products as the customer might require, there were thought to be 'hundreds' of major rivals. By year 2, the firm had narrowed its focus, and there were now thought to be only four serious competitors. However, even with this narrow focus, because of the nature of the industry and the global market in which the firm operated, with new entrants appearing constantly, by year 3 there were thought to be 50–100 major rivals and by the final point of meeting, again there were hundreds. Over this time, competition, as provided by many small firms along with the market leaders, was thought to be 'moderate' at first, falling to 'weak' as the firm repositioned, but rising eventually to 'fierce'.

The products provided by this business were considered by the owner-manager to be generally differentiated, with the exception of year 2, when they were thought to be similar to those of rivals. It was following this second meeting that the owner-manager decided to refocus the business. Goods in the main market in which the firm operated were therefore typically unique, each with its own unique selling point (USP), and no dominant supplier existed. This meant that firms active in this market were subject to fierce competition, constantly having to be aware of the threats posed by incumbents or potential new entrants, as well as meeting the needs of end users of their products by the use of novel and innovative ideas.[2]

---

1 See, for example, Reid et al. (1997), on the effective 'screening' by venture capitalists of potential investees.

2 See Porter's 'Five Forces of Competition' in Porter (1980, p. 4).

Table 6.2: Environment and technology

Year of interview **Age of business**	**Year 1** **30 months**	**Year 2** **45 months**	**Year 3** **56 months**	**Year 4** **70 months**
No. of major rivals	100s	4	50–100	100s
Strength of competition	Moderate	Moderate	Weak	Fierce
Few/many small firms	Many	Many	Many	Many
Differentiated or similar product	Different	Similar	Different	Different
Dominant supplier?	No	No	No	No
Change in processes	Significant	Important	Important	Important
Rivals' change in processes	A lot	?	A little	?
Competitive pressure of process innovation	A lot	None	None	None
No. of new products	6–10	1–5	1–5	0
Rivals' no. of new products	A lot	A little	A lot	A lot
Competitive pressure of product innovation	A lot	None	A lot	A lot
A lot of technical change in the industry?	Yes	Yes	Yes	Yes
Initiators of technical change	Innovators	Market leader(s)	Market leader(s)	Everyone
Key changes in the business		**51 months**: most important change in the business and a move to new premises **56 months**: shortfall in finance needed for strategic purposes **58 months**: new partner – university-trained accountant **71 months**: AIM listing **88-94 months**: main market listing		

6.2.2 *Technological advances*

From the first meeting, this entrepreneur said that significant changes were being made in the business, invariably implemented following his own personal assessment of existing processes. Growth had led the company into different areas and new experiences, requiring new skills and areas of expertise. The firm already had a policy of employing only university graduates, with art, design and music skills, as well as those with the more obvious computing science backgrounds. However, nearly five years into its life cycle, an accounting-trained partner was required and subsequently brought in to oversee the financial management of the business. Technically called the 'chief operations manager', this person was in charge of producing the business plan and ensuring that things ran smoothly on a day-to-day basis.

Generally, where the owner-manager could hazard an answer, he thought that principal rivals undertook 'a lot' of process innovation. However, changes in the *way* they ran their business or produced their goods did not typically put much pressure on his own business. What did put the pressure on were the new products themselves, as they passed out into the marketplace from the manufacturers' production lines. A lot of technical change occurred through the period of this study, initially from innovators in the market, then from market leaders and eventually from all software producers. However, although a great deal of pressure was felt because of this, the entrepreneur had gradually *cut* the number of new products offered each year, from 6–10 in year 1, to 1–5 in years 2 and 3, to none at all in the final year. This reflects the change in the basis on which products were ordered and delivered. Instead of designing new products to sell, the business now sought clients who would commission games, pay a percentage of the royalties up front, and then work alongside them through development, production and marketing. Each product was a single game, commissioned by a software distributor. Long-term product development was now therefore a strategic goal of the firm and, with the added security of these long-term contracts and venture capital backing, the firm could afford to spend longer periods of time on getting the product specification just right.

6.2.3 *Principal or agent?*

Of the many relationships a small-firm owner-manager might have – that of partner, buyer, seller, borrower, lender, and so on – three are of particular interest in an analysis of this specific firm: those between the owner-manager and investors or shareholders; those between the owner-manager and customers; and those between the owner-manager and his workers (Figure 6.1).[3]

3 In acting on behalf of shareholders or customers, the owner-manager acts as an agent. In directing and monitoring his/her workers, the owner-manager acts as a principal, and his/her workers as agents. See also Chapter 5.

Figure 6.1: The owner-manager as principal and agent

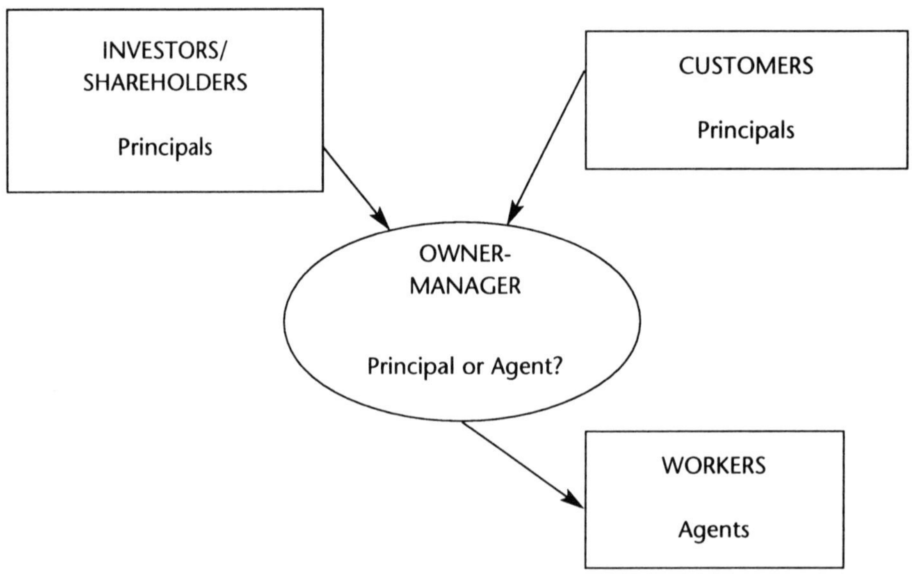

The entrepreneur in this firm could be thought of as acting as an agent to his venture capital investors and other shareholders, the principals (see Reid, 1998). He acted on their behalf, by trying to maximise the return on their investment in his business. The equity investors protected their investments by taking seats on the board and by playing an active role in the running of the firm. They were able to watch closely how their money was being spent, and what was being done to increase the worth of their shareholding, thereby avoiding the information asymmetries that might otherwise arise. This close involvement by the investors would ensure that the entrepreneur did not limit his effort because of the increased security offered by having diluted his equity shareholding. Thus the possible problem of 'moral hazard' in this case was avoided.

This business had an interesting relationship with its customers, who were involved from product inception right through to the end. Again, the entrepreneur could be regarded as an agent of his customers, the principals, who invested up front an advance against royalties, although he considered his firm's relationship with its customers to be 'a partnership', saying that it worked 'hand-in-hand' with them. Customers were reassured about their investment in the business because of their continuous involvement during product development, and were constantly asked for feedback on everything the business was doing, leading to discussions with, and modifications by, personnel in the firm. So again problems of moral hazard and information asymmetry were avoided, through the existence of an open flow of information between the two parties.

The final relationship under consideration here is that of the entrepreneur in this firm with his staff. In this relationship he took the role of principal to his/her workers, the agents. Consider the example of an employee who has no equity stake in the business: his/her inclination will be to exert the minimum effort required to receive a salary cheque at the end of the month. The principal must therefore aim to encourage the effort of his/her agents by installing systems of information provision, monitoring and reward. In this firm, the owner-manager held regular staff, management and board meetings, and took ideas from them in the development of long-term plans. Monitoring took place through a sophisticated computer-based 'time-building system' that costed each job and each employee on an hourly basis. Employees were motivated by the provision of a quality work environment and social events. They were empowered, and given charge of their own work, alongside a negotiated plan of what they should be doing. In addition, they were offered share options and a profit-related bonus. Thus employees were encouraged not to shirk on effort, but instead made to feel that they had a very real stake in the future of the business, and a vested interest in making it a success.

6.2.4 Organisational change

With the increase in employment that this firm had experienced, its organisational structure became more complex. Figure 6.2 displays the change in hierarchy within the business over the four years during which it was examined. To begin with, the firm had a very simple structure as a sole trader, with the owner-manager at level one controlling his three employees at level two. By the second time of interview, limited company status brought with it a third level of hierarchy and additional employees. This was consolidated in year 3, with personnel being added at all levels, and by the final year of interview, a fourth level of hierarchy was added, as the business became a public company and more than doubled its personnel.

The owner-manager summarised his changing role as follows:

> At the start, I did everything, including making the tea. Now I do business development and long-term business planning. I *never* work on the product any more. I sit with teams and have discussions and operational input; but my main role is now strategic planning and generating new business. You have to trust the people you're bringing in and let them get on with it.

Obviously, such changes bring with them implications for the exercising of authority by superiors over their subordinates. Initially, this was a basic operational process: the owner-manager was in charge, and he told people what to do. By the second interview, there was still not thought to be a recognised system of authority. However, by year 3, it was apparent that superior staff could intervene selectively at lower levels to exercise authority. And the system had become more clearly and formally defined by year 4: with the four levels of hierarchy in place, superiors now had authority only over their immediate subordinates.

In terms of the division of labour within the business, originally there was little distinction between the employees, who would work together with the joint sole aim of producing the goods. However, over time, as more personnel were brought in, the workers began to take responsibility for their own individual areas of specialisation. So their tasks became first 'reasonably clearly', and then 'exactly', defined. However,

Figure 6.2: Changing hierarchical pyramid of the firm over time

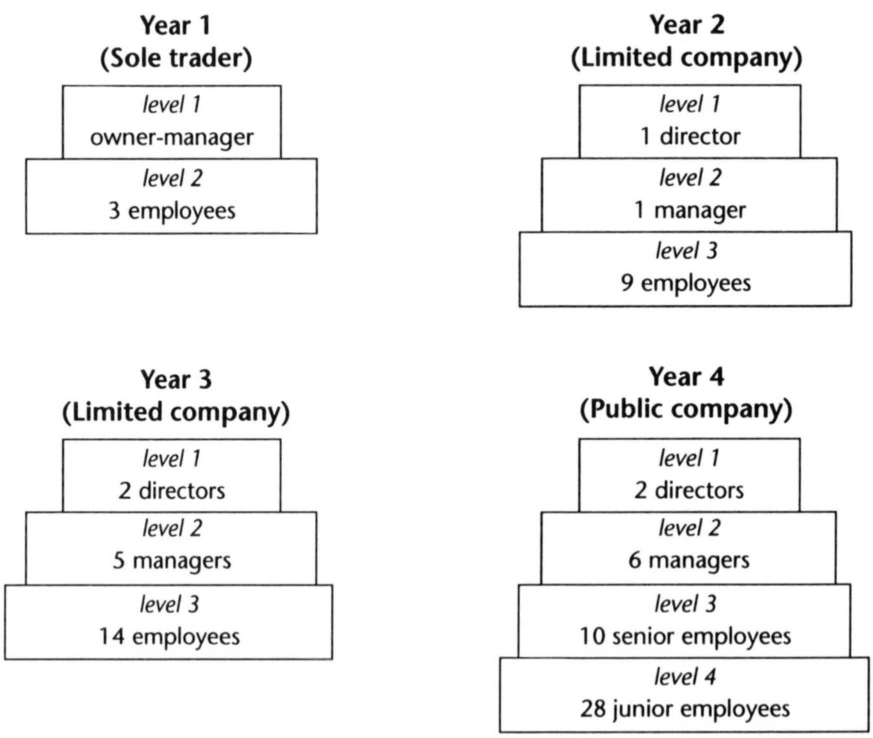

contrary to what one might anticipate, with this clearer distinction between roles also came the expectation that workers would, when the need arose, take over each others' tasks. So alongside an increasing skills and knowledge base came a growing awareness of the need for flexibility and task-sharing.

With the increasing numbers, growth in complexity and greater flexibility now established, the communication of procedures took on greater importance. Thus every process was documented on the computer, available for anyone to consult, as and when required. In fact, 'everything' was held on the PC. As the owner-manager said, 'I couldn't imagine any other way. It would be impossible without PCs, for the speed they can turn around a budget when we feed in real information. We would need a team of accountants otherwise'.

6.2.5 Management accounting system

This business had experienced a great deal of change in its young life. It was in a highly competitive and technologically advanced market, with the need for continued innovation being crucial to its survival and success. Quick and reliable information was of prime importance to decision-making, and it is to this that we now turn. We shall see how the management accounting system in the firm was developed in response to the above demands for information and the factors covered in the preceding sections of this discussion.

Accounting information had been prepared within the firm by the new university-trained director for one year, and additionally by a professional accounting clerk for six months. The latter had over twenty years of experience in preparing business accounts. About one-fifth of the director's time in a week was spent on this task. The business produced full management accounts on a monthly basis, and regularly set budgets or targets for the profit and loss, balance sheet, cash flow and bank balance. All these were regarded as very important to the management of the firm, except for the profit and loss account, which was currently thought to be only slightly important.

Capital investments were typically evaluated through a process of qualitative assessment linked to the personnel involved in a particular project, rather than through any quantitative measure of, say, return on investment. However, the business had made use of modern accounting practices (such as activity-based costing) and value analysis, since its inception. Thus it was able to produce information segmented by product, by division or workgroup, and by customer.

With such an obviously PC-based organisation, it is unsurprising that computer software was used extensively to handle information within this business. Thus it was used to store data, for financial modelling, for forecasting and for sensitivity analysis. Again, this had been in place since the business had started. Managers were not privy to such information, which was all handled 'at the top', i.e. at board level. Many factors had influenced the development of accounting information within this firm. These included growth in sales and the number of employees; the experiencing of problems in performance; the increasing complexity of the operational process; and the introduction of new capital, primarily through venture capital investment.

The accounting information produced by this firm was used extensively in the running of the business. For example, in terms of planning and analysis, it was used:

- to help the business keep within budget;
- to identify productivity-raising opportunities;
- to reach specified levels of output;
- to analyse business performance against projected values;
- to justify proposed expenditure;
- to measure the performance of teams of employees.

In terms of activating and directing daily operations, the accounting information generated was used:

- to evaluate product performance;
- to calculate the effects of marginal changes in costs and revenue;
- to identify operations which have become inefficient;
- to measure the speed of production.

Finally, as regards the complexity of the use of accounting information within this business, the owner-manager thought that it helped, in terms of problem-solving and decision-making:

- to evaluate or choose between alternative actions;
- to assess a new project or investment;

- to set prices;
- to analyse the riskiness of a new idea;
- to decide whether to replace old assets with new assets;
- to determine the number of products to produce;
- to determine the remuneration of staff.

The information so produced was considered to be 'totally reliable, if idiosyncratic', and the owner-manager declared that he had no difficulty in making sense or use of the accounting information available to him.

6.2.6 Conclusions for Case Study A

The management accounting system within this business was well structured, detailed and accurate, reflecting the needs of its users. For example, investors would require regular management accounts, customers would want to know how their money was being spent on production, and management would need an up-to-date analysis of income and expenditure. Thus the sophisticated computing system, which had been in place to begin with, had grown and developed over time in response to these requirements. Further, two new staff had been employed within the last year, their purpose being to concentrate on providing and analysing accounting information in a more detailed way than previously.

The firm's ability to use such information in the daily running of the business was reflected, most obviously, in its continued success, as regards sales, and in the evidence of a hard-working, happy and motivated workforce. This is consistent with, for example, the finding of Raymond and Magnenat-Thalmann (1982, p.25) that 'computer-based information systems have had a noticeable impact on small companies at the operations level'. Thus it has been shown that changes in the firm's environment, its use of technology, its organisational form, and its relationships with parties both within and outside the business, can lead to modifications to its management accounting system. An improvement in information so generated can help businesses such as this to focus their efforts on achieving growth and success.

6.3 Case Study B: Cable and electromechanical assemblies

The company was established in 1991 by the three directors, who operated from home as cable and electromechanical assemblers. They provided all of the initial capital, and the company ownership was divided equally among the directors, with each of their wives also having a small holding. All three had experience of the industry, having been employees of other companies operating in the sector.

Targeting a market niche in portable and mobile telecoms, the company was extremely successful from the outset. From an initial annual turnover of approximately £40,000 the business experienced four years of rapid growth. Staffing increased to in excess of 40, dedicated work premises were obtained, annual sales exceeded £1 million and a high level of profitability was achieved. However, during the last two years financial performance had dipped markedly, with sales almost halving and the firm returning to a break-even level of profit. A majority of the staff were laid off. Table 6.3 illustrates this pattern of strong growth and decline through some key statistics.

Table 6.3: Key statistics of the business

	Year 1	Year 2	Year 3	Year 4
Directors	3	3	3	2
Managers/supervisors	Nil	3	2	Nil
Full-time staff	29	35	10	12
Part-time staff	8	4	Nil	Nil
Trainees	1	Nil	Nil	Nil
Legal form	Private limited company	Private limited company	Private limited company	Private limited company
No. products (groups)	2	2	2	1
Turnover	£1.1m	£1.3m	£0.67m	£0.6m
Net profit	£220,000	£200,000	£nil	£nil

During this latter period of decline the firm changed from having an explicit growth in market share objective and formal written plans expressed in financial terms, to a more modest aim of 'stabilising the company after a bad year' and some broad business objectives which simply exist 'in the head' of the owner-manager.

The company operated in a highly competitive market categorised as either 'strong' or 'fierce' by the owner-manager (Table 6.4). The number of competitors exhibited a strong rise as the pressure of competition became manifest in deteriorating financial performance. The survival and success depended on the provision of a high-quality product at a low price. Consequently, there was continuous pressure to improve productivity in order to maintain both price competitiveness and profitability. Although there was little technical differentiation possible at the product level, much of the initial growth of the firm was due to the firm's ability to provide an overall service, which resulted in a high level of customer satisfaction. In particular, the speed of response by the firm and its speed in completing work was considered a key factor in its success. Its reputation grew as its quality reputation was spread among customers, largely by word of mouth. New business was obtained and an ability to hang on to existing customers compounded the turnover growth. However, as competitors began to match the levels of service provided by the firm and economic conditions in the sector worsened, business became harder to win and two years of decline followed.

It is notable that the business was labour- rather than capital-intensive. Its finance came from the original capital contributions of the directors and the profits ploughed back from the first four successful years.

Table 6.4: Market forces

	Year 1 (38 months)	Year 2 (50 months)	Year 3 (62 months)	Year 4 (76 months)
No. of major rivals	6	10	50	50
Strength of competition	Strong	Fierce	Strong	Fierce
Few/many small firms	Similar	Similar	Similar	Similar
Is there a dominant supplier/competitor in market?	Yes	No	No	No
Change in processes	Significant	Significant	No change	No change
Rivals' change in processes	A lot	Don't know	None	None
Competitive pressure of process innovation	A little	None	None	None
No. of new products	6–10	1–5	None	1–5
Rivals' no. of new products	Don't know	None	Little	Little
Competitive pressure of product innovations	A little	None	Little	Little
A lot of technological change in the industry?	Yes	No	No	No
Initiators of technological change	Market leaders	N/A	N/A	N/A

6.3.1 Technological conditions

The first five years of the company's existence were associated with considerable technological change. This related both to internal business processes and to the firm's product outputs. Indeed, these two aspects of change were linked as the development of new product innovations had required significant changes in technical work processes. These were initiated largely by the directors and transmitted through 'on-the-job training' to the other employers. The accounting and planning processes were computerised and use was made of a database to maintain information on the business. New product development had been a marked aspect of the business until the last two years, and the technical know-how of competitors had been rated a strong threat. Technological advantage was important but could not be protected to give durability to the benefits. It was something to be exploited quickly, as others would soon copy any improvements made. Monitoring competitors' work methods and products was an important part of the competitive dynamics in this market.

During the last two years innovation decreased with no change in work processes and no new products being introduced. The company had begun to seek out work where it simply operated to specifications set by its customers.

6.3.2 Organisation

The owner-managers of the firm (three directors from inception till 1997, two thereafter) had adopted a 'hands-on' policy in the day-to-day running of the firm from the start and continued the policy throughout the growth and decline phases of the firm. By 1995, however, they had introduced an intermediate level of supervisor/manager to help cope with supervision of 35 staff (see Table 6.3), although this did not restrict the directors' readiness to have direct managerial contact with all staff.

The firm required technically competent employees but tried not to hire 'narrow specialists'. Specific training was 'on the job', and consequently most of the employees had a good knowledge of the tasks of others. In this way a highly flexible workforce was maintained. As employee remuneration was a significant cost element it was necessary to promote and ensure that their technical skills and performance were of a high level. This was a major source of the productivity improvement which enabled competitiveness to be maintained. The development of employee skill and application was therefore a critical factor in the company's success. Formal annual performance appraisals were given to all staff until 1997, although in that year quarterly informal appraisals were also in use. However, by 1998 the shrinkage in firm size had resulted in the abandonment of the appraisal system.

6.3.3 Management accounting

Despite the turbulence caused by the large and fast movements in company size, the internal accounting system exhibited considerable stability. To a large extent this appeared to be due to the establishment of a core system on day one which proved to be robust enough to cope with the changes experienced. This system was based on the standard *Sage* package and generated monthly profit and loss accounts and balance sheets together with breakdown analyses of income and costs. In addition, the package allowed cash-flow statements and the bank balance to be monitored on a weekly basis. While all of this information was considered useful, the profit and cash-flow information was rated of high importance in running the firm. Indeed, management accounting in general was taken extremely seriously as the managing director observed that it had been a 'day-one' development and he explained that 'we take great care to put information correctly into our system'. The architect of this provision was the wife of one of the directors, who had considerable experience in bank administration and who worked part-time for the company. Further support came from the external accountants who prepared the company's statutory accounts. The owner-manager's understanding of accounting had been considerably enhanced by the explanations provided in question-and-answer sessions with his accountant.

The firm's strategic outlook was based on maintaining a low cost base. The need to enhance productivity to remain competitive ensured that cost information was a major part of information flow. The two largest costs elements were material (35 per cent of total cost) and labour (also 35 per cent of total cost). Consequently, these were monitored closely. Material was assessed in relation to sales income, with targets established of what this percentage should be for each job as a control. Alternative material supply prices were also closely reviewed, but it was appreciated that the quality of materials used was an important component of overall quality and this could not be compromised. Labour, time and cost analysis were provided by the software package, and this gave important information for the assessment of individual employee performance, the opportunities for future improvements and the identification of where to target downsizing decisions. This information assisted the business in maintaining the flexibility of these two cost elements as sales varied. The gross profit percentage was used as an indicator of success in achieving this aim. On overhead cost, only normal accounting listings were produced and, at the level of the individual job, overheads were identified by means of a percentage added to the direct costs. Cost measurement was done on an actual basis expectation of a material cost/sales relationship and a gross profit percentage.

Accounting information thus contributed in a variety of ways to the direction of day-to-day operations. Specifically, the managing director identified its role in:

- identification of trends in important business variables;
- assessing and managing stock levels;
- evaluating performance on jobs;
- identification of cost and revenue variations;
- measurement of work time.

While planning had become less formal in recent years because of the massive variations in turnover, there remained the directors' 'rules of thumb' in respect of the gross profit percentage, targets for material cost and for profit on specific jobs, and close analysis of the performance of employees. All of these were used to try to control costs by identifying (a) when the need to improve productivity arose and (b) the opportunity for doing so.

Decision-making was also influenced by accounting. Initially, the business as a whole had been assessed on the basis of the return it would generate on the initial investment, and projected cash flows had allowed an internal rate of return and payback period to be completed. These methods were retained for use when considering asset replacements. While many key operational decisions (e.g. pricing, output levels, product development) were determined by circumstances independent of accounting, the major decision of whether or not to shut down all or part of the business was kept under review by examining and monitoring ongoing profitability and cash flow.

6.3.4 Conclusions for Case Study B

This case study illustrates how a managerial accounting system can exhibit little change despite existing within the context of a set of highly dynamic economic and organisational circumstances. Periods of rapid growth and decline, changes in organisational structure and intensely competitive conditions had little effect on internal accounting. This appears to be largely because of the seriousness with which the company directors took the issue of information provision at the inception of the firm. Considerable care was taken in the installation of a monthly financial statement reporting package and a daily cash monitoring system when the firm commenced. These were seen as the fundamentals which would facilitate effective management, and maintenance of the established system was an administrative priority. It was an approach which supported the firm through four highly successful years. Moreover, it may be viewed as a contributory factor to the firm's ability to cope with a period of sharp decline. The need for, the means of and the success of their downsizing policies were all made apparent from the management accounting reports. Consequently, it is unsurprising that the directors considered that the accounting system generated both reliable and highly useful information.

6.4 Case Study C: Contract joinery (carpentry) specialists

This company had been in business about two and a half years before the first site visit (year 1). The basic skills deployed within the business were good-quality joinery (i.e. carpentry) work, and the main customers for its services were typically retail- and leisure-based. The specific contracts concluded with customers varied from the refurbishment of a sheriff court to the fabrication of an airport check-in. The workforce remained fairly stable over the four years, averaging around 50 full-time employees, but the managerial side experienced considerable growth. In the first year it was examined, this firm had had only one manager but, by the fourth year, it had acquired a further six. This increase in hierarchy was probably a reflection of the very much increased volume of trade, and therefore the increased need for monitoring and control. From a gross figure of £2.1m in year 1, turnover grew steadily year by year, to £2.0m, £3.9m and finally £5m in year 4. This represents an annual growth rate in sales of 35 per cent.[4]

6.4.1 Dynamics of growth and change

A main feature of interest in this case study is how the firm coped with greatly increased sales, but stable scale, and, at the same time, stable extent and composition of its workforce. Another feature of its stability was a constant focus on Britain as the main market. However, the dynamics of rapid sales growth were associated with many changes. Although the major rivals were always perceived to be small (typically fewer than 10), the total numbers of rivals were widely estimated as running to hundreds or even thousands over the years the firm was examined. Market share was always small (usually less than 3 per cent), though by year 4 it was estimated at 4 per cent. This suggests a rapidly growing market overall, within which the firm faced a constant core of main rivals, but a vast and volatile array of minor rivals, against all of which it achieved a slight competitive edge over time.

The perceived level of competitiveness had increased markedly between years 1 and 4. Initially, competition was thought to be strong only as regards price, volume and salesmanship. By year 4, strong competitiveness had extended to include quality, design, customisation and after-sales care. In years 2 and 3, strong additional competitive pressures were felt from technical progressiveness and advertising. Technical progressiveness in the industry as a whole was not perceived to be great for much of the

4 Growth rates of 38 per cent, 34 per cent and 28 per cent between the four years.

firm's existence, but had been very marked in the early years of the firm. Then, new government regulations on quality and safety had provided a major stimulus to the market as a whole, as customers demanded refitting to meet these new regulations. Thus new demands for safer and higher-quality fittings were generated. These factors probably go a very long way towards explaining the significant volume of new trade that the company enjoyed.

6.4.2 External information

In terms of external information, a wide class of information sources was regarded as important by the firm. Questions were posed about searching for technical knowledge which was relevant to new products and processes. It was found that, in year 1, trade journals, government bodies, suppliers and customers were regarded as very important, with licensed technologies, consultants and rival firms also being regarded as important. As the four years in which the company was examined progressed, fewer information sources were ranked as being highly important (only trade journals and customers by year 4), though most sources continued to be regarded as important. This suggests that inception and early growth for the firm were indeed associated with exogenous change of the sort considered by contingency theory. As time progressed, the consequences of these exogenous changes were worked through by the firm in terms of external information requirements and, ultimately, evolving organisational form.

Feedback from customers was an important source of information, and it was both asked for and freely given. This feedback was used for referral later, for discussion with customers and to implement changes based on their suggestions. One of the directors interviewed commented, 'we use their comments to promote the business'. Here, customer feedback is being used positively to enhance advertising messages. In its early years, the company did not gather trade intelligence on its rivals. But by year 2 (four years after inception) the firm was actively gathering trade intelligence on rivals. This process was wide ranging, extending from market share and new products to product quality, customer relations, marketing methods and pricing. Such information was usually collected frequently (typically at monthly intervals). The means of gathering information were diverse, an exhaustive list being electronic databases, government publications, trade journals, library sources, newspapers, membership of trade associations – not excluding good old-fashioned business 'schmooze' – personal enquiry and conversations.

However, at this stage, the firm had a low IT intensity. Year 3 saw a similar picture on the gathering of trade intelligence, with 'the grapevine' being added to information sources. However, a radical difference in IT usage was emerging by year 3 – it suddenly become very important. A broad range of IT devices or techniques was in use: phone, fax, telephone answering machine, telephone conferencing facility, cellular telephone, personal computer and electronic database. These IT devices were used for many purposes, including tracking competitors, designing new products and networking. They were also important for internal monitoring and control and were used to produce accounts for administration, for forecasting, and for producing business plans. A similar level of IT intensity was evident in year 4, but by now its importance had been reduced from 'very' to 'moderately' important. An increase in IT intensity is often associated with an increase in scale, scope and complexity of data. Here, it seemed to follow on from the rapid rise in access to trade intelligence-gathering. It also corresponded (see below) with the introduction of modern production practices within the firm.

6.4.3 Internal information

In terms of internal information generation, the firm had the benefit of a college-trained accountant who had worked within the firm since a year after its inception. This person was the principal preparer of accounting information within the firm, to which task 70 per cent of the working week was allocated. Targets (or budgets) and outcomes were set for profit and loss, balance sheet, cash flow and bank balance, all of which were rated as important or highly important to the running of the firm. Profit and loss and balance sheet were measured quarterly and the cash flow and bank balance monthly.[5] Thus the general picture presented is of a small firm which is information intensive.

Considerable evolution had occurred over the lifetime of the business, in terms of the purposes to which internal information was turned. As regards formal decision-making about capital investment, the firm was using a return on investment measure soon after inception. After a further year, this was supplemented with a payback period decision rule on investment. Cost management too was subject to evolution. Modern accounting practices were adopted within a year and a half of inception, to be augmented by value analysis (i.e. identifying which activities did not add value) six months after that. Five years after inception (year 3), modern production practices were adopted. The latter was a major internal development, and no doubt accounted for both the continued sales increases of £1m and £1.1m between years 2 and 4, and to an even more conspicuous extent the marked increases in labour productivity.[6] This was £52.7k per person in year 3, and had risen to £102k per person by year 4. This was a remarkable doubling of labour productivity between the fifth and seventh year of the company's existence. These absolute levels of labour productivity are also high, in relation to norms established by large dataset studies elsewhere.

In terms of information flows within the business, the firm was in that minority of firms in the sample which thought of its business as being decomposable into parts. In this case, information flows around the firm were split up by product and by work group. This is a modern conception of information flows within the firm, and indeed, as Jordan (1989) has argued, is a prerequisite to efficient managerial control and decision-making, especially in terms of the pursuit of long-run profit. The firm's information flows had been treated this way from inception.

5 The data of this paragraph relate to year 4 for the firm.

6 Here measured by sales ÷ full-time workforce.

Spreadsheets and other computer software had been used within the business from inception. Initially, this was just to store information. After a year, it was extended to project appraisal, then to financial modelling a year later. Further along the line (year 1), software was put into use for forecasting and simulation purposes. In other words, information handling became increasingly sophisticated as the firm grew in size. The fact that the business had always been thought of as being made up of parts suggests that the initial conception of the business was that it was well above the micro-firm size. Its growth history corresponds to what David Birch (1996) has called 'gazelles'. These are firms that enjoy startlingly high growth right from inception, and continue to grow steadily year by year until a large desired or optimum firm size is achieved.

6.4.4 Accounting information system

The management within the firm received regular accounting information on matters of obvious importance, like performance, budget targets and the financial implications of specific decisions, but also on less obvious matters like tender structure and their profitability. Information had developed significantly over time. In particular, it had become more detailed. The director we interviewed told us that 'joinery [carpentry] work is now broken down into five disciplines. We make sure that *each* of these meet required margins (and they differ!).' Many factors had influenced the introduction or development of accounting information within the firm, including sales growth, organisational change and the introduction of new capital. At a less obvious level, employee growth (notably in management) and product growth (notably in hotel refurbishment) were also important. This increase in the detail of accounting provision increased the directors' confidence in the reliability of accounting information. The director who was interviewed said, 'we've developed our own system over the years, and "fine tuned" it. It was maybe 50 per cent reliable five years ago, but now it is at least 90 per cent reliable.' Perhaps as a consequence, there were no perceived difficulties in using accounting information in the firm.

When asked what accounting information was used for in the business, under the headings of 'Effective planning and analysis', 'Activation and direction of daily operations', and 'Problem-solving and decision-making', the director's responses made it clear that the information used was highly complex. Almost all categories under each of the three broad headings above, numbering 30 in all, were evaluated by the director as being relevant to information use by the firm. It was noticeable, too, that the few categories not mentioned were often in areas where the firm was so abundantly successful that they were perhaps not thought worth mentioning. Examples of this include identifying productivity-raising opportunities (under 'effective planning and analysis'), ensuring product conformity to quality standards (under 'activation and direction') and determining the optimal number of products (under 'problem-solving and decision-making'). The labour productivity figures reported above speak for themselves in terms of high performance. Quality standards (arising from government legislation) in a sense created the markets for this business in the first place. The firm had been most successful in identifying hotel refurbishment as a major new product (taking over from retail outlet fitting). Thus the overall picture that emerges is of the firm implementing very complex information systems.

6.4.5 *Use of hierarchy for monitoring and control*

Variations in the hierarchical nature of the firm were apparently not marked, yet these were noteworthy when they appeared. At the level of full-time employees, change was actually quite slight, year by year. The business steadily averaged around 50 employees at this level for most of its existence. However, managers grew from just one in year 1 to seven in year 4. The salary multiple between the full-time worker level and managerial level was 1.75 in year 1, 2.0 in year 2 and 2.0 in year 3. It then shifted markedly to 4.0 in year 4, which also corresponded to a sharp rise in the management team, from two to seven. This suggests that the desire for greater control and performance, in the face of rapid growth, led to a more incentivised remuneration structure, and a more 'peaked' or 'deep' hierarchy.

The private company form was retained throughout all the years that the firm had been in existence. However, there were significant differences over time in the way the firm was run. Initially, authority was allowed to be exercised selectively at lower levels. Discretion over subordinates was considerable, monitoring was discretionary and unpredictable, and superiors mostly got subordinates to understand and act on what was wanted. In other words, the administrative structure was informal and compliance was high. By year 4 (6½ years old), authority was only to be exercised through the next level down, rather than selectively. Discretion had become merely extensive, rather than considerable. Monitoring had become standard (rather than discretionary) and occurred at regular (rather unpredictable) intervals. Superiors now frequently (rather than mostly) got subordinates to understand and act on their instructions. Thus, there was clearly a sharp tightening up in the operation of hierarchy in the firm as growth occurred. Most of this happened towards the end of the period examined (year 4), but many signs of it were evident earlier. For example, by year 2, selective intervention had been ruled out, and by year 3 monitoring had become regular, rather than unpredictable. In short, as the firm grew, and with it its information system became more complex, monitoring became more precise and the exercise of control more evident.

6.4.6 *Agency effects*

Some obvious agency effects are apparent in hierarchy as it operated in the business, which is not surprising as hierarchy can be regarded as a form of tiered principal–agent relations. However, some specifically agency-governed effects were observed, which are worthy of comment. In the early years, compliance was no problem between manager and worker. Non-compliance mainly arose from unclear instructions, subordinate indiscipline, superior indiscipline or dissatisfaction with work or pay conditions. Dismissal was a matter for directors only and it was rarely used for disciplinary reasons. Then, five years from inception (year 2), dismissals started to be handled at a lower hierarchical level. After this restructuring, disciplinary problems became much more evident, and accounted for one-quarter of dismissals (year 2). By year 3, such problems were even more in evidence, and as much as three-quarters of dismissals were on disciplinary grounds. By this point, monitoring was much more systematic and structured. By year 4, unclear instructions had become irrelevant as a source of non-compliance, and loyalty conflicts had crept into the list of causes. Dismissal had become strictly a second-level management issue[7] (rather than being the concern of directors alone) and the main cause was disciplinary problems (75 per cent). What seems to have happened is that more rigorous monitoring had reduced information asymmetry. Thus perks, non-compliance, or low effort, which may not even have been observed before, were now being detected, and were increasingly being driven out. As a consequence, moral hazard was attenuated by the increased use of dismissal if performance defaults were severe. Management powers were beefed up to achieve this, both in terms of a jump in the size of the managerial team and in terms of a marked increase in the relative pay of managers. At the same time, directors, as 'peak co-ordinators', developed more concern for strategic issues, as opposed to operational issues. This became possible because they had become insulated from issues of 'putting out fires' such as dismissal issues, as responsibility for these was pushed further down the organisational pyramid.

The last year (year 4) in which the firm was examined corresponded to the one important period in its history in which it had implemented new technology. At the beginning, the firm was a rather informally organised business, which used relatively little IT. Its authority structure was loose, permitting much forgiveness in the face of performance default, and using only basic monitoring. Over time, the business became transformed into an IT-intensive firm, with stringent monitoring, tight organisation and little forgiveness for performance default. The level of information usage, both internal and external, increased rapidly over just a few years, and all these factors seem to have accounted for the remarkable record of labour productivity achieved within the firm.

6.4.7 Conclusions for Case Study C

Case Study C illustrates how a constant firm size, in terms of employment, can yet be associated with rapid sales growth, organisational evolution and information system complexity. The firm achieved good economic performance, and this was attended by more sophisticated information handling on several levels. First, external information was drawn into the business from multifarious sources, from the informal to formal. This was associated with a rapid rise in the intensity of IT use within the firm. It became 'information intensive'. Second, the provision and use of internal information evolved considerably over this firm's life cycle. Shortly after inception, modern accounting practices were adopted within the firm, which itself was analysed in a decomposed, rather than unitary, fashion. The accounting information available in this firm was extensive and detailed, and had developed significantly over time. Use of hierarchy to enhance monitoring and control had been extensively adopted, and generally successfully implemented. Agency effects had emerged, and steps were

7 Though the managerial ethos on dismissal was said to be influenced by the directors.

taken to deal with non-compliance. This was handled by increased authority being vested in principals, and more highly incentivised pay structures.

6.5 Overall conclusions from case studies

This chapter has presented three case studies to illustrate the application of our three theories to specific firms from our sample. We have seen how problems of moral hazard and information asymmetry may be confronted and overcome, through increased monitoring and supervision. We have seen also that relationships, organisational change and the theory of markets v. hierarchies might have an impact upon the introduction and development of a firm's management information system. And we have presented evidence to show that the firm's accounting information may be used to help the business in overcoming any problems and in making sensible operational and strategic decisions pertinent to the running of the firm.

Some insights may also be obtained, from these three cases, into the practical evolution of management accounting in the small firm. It was apparent that the importance and success attributed to management accounting in the firms was derived from an investment of time and effort in designing and developing a coherent and useful accounting information flow to management. In Case B this took place largely in the very early stages of the firm's inception, so that the system established would cope with future organisational change. However, in Cases A and C, management accounting was progressively developed over time, in response to the key variables of growth in size and scope of operations, and variation in staffing and organisational structure.

Notably, in all of the firms, specialist administrative and accounting staff were dedicated to the accounting function. While traditional accounting reports (profit and loss accounts and cash-flow statements) were central to the systems developed, there was a recognition that these needed frequent reporting (weekly in Case B and monthly in Cases A and C). In order to achieve this with limited commitment of staff time, the key aspects of the management accounting systems in the three firms were computerised. This characteristic of the accounting systems also facilitated one other important and common facet of the information flow, i.e. the focus on specific jobs.

Once again, in all three cases, there was a clear managerial demand for cost and revenue information on the detailed components of the work profile of the firm. Profitability of the individual job or product was viewed as the building block for firm success. Even though the reliability of information on this aspect of performance could be questioned (Case C), its importance was evidenced by the efforts made to ensure that this drawback was overcome and by the significance afforded it by the firm's owner-manager.

Finally, the flourishing nature of management accounting in these firms reflects its championing by the key management players. Their support for the necessary investment and ongoing prominent utilisation of information outputs helped to ensure that management accounting had become a practical and highly regarded service within their organisations.

7

Conclusion

7.1 Overview

The study of the development, use and importance of management accounting in a small-firm context is one which has received only limited research attention. Occasional, rather than sustained and comprehensive, inquiry is an appropriate description of the current position, and rigorous analytical work is conspicuous by its scarcity. This neglect is not justifiable on economic grounds, given the size and importance of this form of organisation to most national economies. Nor is it reflective of any lack of significance of internal accounting information to the management of this type of organisation. Thus, the studies which have been undertaken suggest that accounting information can be an influential factor in affecting managerial performance. Further, it is valued by small-firm management, and this is confirmed by our own work.

The small-firm setting has been shown to be one with many research advantages for those interested in understanding the evolution and role of management accounting within organisations. It offers visibility for the subject of study and an environment where prominent contingencies, such as extensive and rapid growth, performance variation, technological investment and organisational and managerial structure, are all contributors to substantial circumstantial changes. These have considerable implications for the provision of management accounting.

In this study we have reviewed the existing literature relevant to the supply and use of management accounting within the small firm. This has emphasised both internal and external information, and the importance of IT-based systems. We have extended prior research on the topic by using three economics-based organisational theories (contingency theory, agency theory, and markets v. hierarchies) as a framework for explaining the dynamics of management accounting development in small firms. Evidence of two types has been used to substantiate and exemplify the theoretical basis of the study. First, the data collected from a sample of over 80 Scottish small firms was reviewed and then analysed statistically to ascertain the extent to which the theories were supported empirically. Second, three case studies were presented to complement this quantitative, aggregate analysis with a more qualitative and detailed description of the key variables and their operation *vis-à-vis* management accounting. Although the empirical data gathered can, and have been, used descriptively to provide a review of the nature of management accounting in small firms, it is perhaps even more significant that, from this work, a number of overlapping conclusions can be drawn in relation to the fundamental issues of *why* management accounting exists within the small firm, on *how* it develops in this setting, on *what* functions it fulfils and on the *difficulties* which may be encountered in understanding and prescribing practice in this area. These are presented below under the four headings of significance, variation, explanatory factors and prescription and policy implications. A final section suggesting future research opportunities is also provided.

7.2 Significance

Existing research suggests that the management accounting system of the small firm has a significant effect on the operation and performance of the business. Management accounting practice is thus an important issue for small firms. In theory, this relationship can be attributed to the constructive use of management accounting information to support monitoring behaviour by owner-managers as the firm grows (particularly through the institution of formal planning systems) and its enhancement of decision-making by addressing the problems of coping with uncertainty and assisting 'feedforward' activities.

This study confirms that the development of management accounting in the small firm is influenced significantly by key events and contingencies. Consequently, their identification and prediction can assist in the design and modification of management accounting practice. For example, staffing growth, the introduction of a management hierarchy and the emergence of new competition may all be factors which should trigger changes in management accounting.

This research also confirms the extensive use of management accounting information in small firms. Budgets, costing, cost management techniques and financial performance indicators were all widely evident among the research subjects and were used to activate and direct operations and to influence a broad range of key decisions. Moreover, a general analysis of the data gathered indicated that low-performing small firms engaged in less planning and financial analysis than their more successful counterparts.

However, our results also indicate that the impact of management accounting is greatest in the small firm which is struggling to survive (where it can provide a day-to-day monitoring of finances and help identify trends in key variables such as cash flow, sales and stock levels) and in those which are enjoying success (where management accounting can help both to direct growth and to cope with the administrative and control burdens which it brings). In those firms where financial performance is satisfactory, although somewhat static, less importance is attributed to the provision of management accounting information.

Finally, the research undertaken provides significant evidence to support the conceptualisation of small-firm development in terms of the three economic theories used as a framework for the study. However, it is also notable that these theories are in many ways closely related, and that they offer considerable overlap and mutual support as economic explanations for the creation of systems to supply accounting information within small firms.

7.3 Variation

Firms comprising the small-firm sector should not be considered to be homogeneous. There is considerable variation among small firms in terms of key factors which influence their management accounting systems. Size, performance, growth rates, managerial expertise and sectoral location are all examples of factors which ensure a lack of universality in appropriate small-firm management accounting. Prior research also confirms the influence of these variables on the information supplied for both planning and decision-making. Moreover, the case studies recounted in Chapter 6 provide detailed descriptions of how different circumstances conspire to produce different types of internal information system. Variation is also particularly evident but specifiable in the use of statistical analysis to identify different firm typologies which characterise the different natures and roles for management accounting. These range from the more formal and structured use of information to the relative neglect or, at best, informal use of financial information.

7.4 Explanatory factors

This study has provided support for a range of factors which seem to provide explanations for the variation found in small-firm management accounting systems and practices. In accord with traditional contingency theory, the competitiveness of the market environment was found to have a marked influence on organisational scale. In addition, significant relationships were found between the timescale of decision-planning activities, the sophistication of product costing systems and firm size. However, the influence of technology (an important contingent variable for larger firms) was not found to be important for small firms. These findings are also of some importance for the validation of agency and markets v. hierarchies theories. The dependent variable used as a characterisation of the organisation was based on a weighting of staff numbers. This measure captured both the extended scope of the moral hazard problem identified in agency theory which creates the need for accounting monitoring information, and the consequences of the creation or expansion of internal hierarchies to cope with the organisation of staff, thus creating a need for new information flows.

Some (albeit weak) explanation of management accounting complexity or sophistication was also found in the organisational characteristic of sub-unit interdependence, a factor which is indicative of the segmentation of the organisation. Once again, this is a factor which can exacerbate the agency problem and encourage the adoption of a hierarchical organisation structure. Additionally, the existence of an incentivising remuneration system based on performance was found to have a strong association with more highly developed and complex management accounting. The incentivisation needed to combat moral hazard thus appears to create a demand for a management accounting system which can adequately support the necessary monitoring and performance measurements.

Finally, a positive relationship was found between the volume of information provided for planning activity and the amount of feedback on actual performance. This is indicative not merely of monitoring behaviour but of the type of information support necessary to maintain viable management within a hierarchical structure. These results indicate the strength of the economic motive in the small-firm context, and this underlies the fit which contingency, agency and markets v. hierarchies achieve with the empirical data.

7.5 Prescription and policy implications

The results of this study indicate that the idea of general prescriptions for the management accounting systems of small firms is inappropriate. Sources of variation in organisation characteristics and circumstances (see above sections) should be considered as fundamental to management accounting system design. Indeed, there is some recognition of this in the most recent professional prescriptive guidance (see IFAC/CIMA, 1998). The advice is provided in terms of a long checklist of information possibilities, so that alternative packages of information may be selected as appropriate. However, there is no indication in this publication of the factors which might determine specific information suitability, and in this respect empirical studies of the type undertaken are of value. The document's contents are also consistent with the advocacy of a supply of information for small-firm management which reflects external conditions. This is one area which has received strong support in previous research and is also supported by this study's findings. In terms of information categorisation, it is best represented as *strategic management accounting*. The small firm may often, because of its size and lack of financial backing, operate in a precarious position. If management are to appreciate this situation and react to it, they need information which sets their own performance and outlook in the context of their competitors' performance, their current market position and the prospects for the sector in which they operate. In this respect, there may be a role for trade associations or government support agencies to produce relevant contextual information on specific market conditions and to organise regular sectoral benchmarking exercises for small firms. The provision of this information in a form suitable for tailored software incorporation would also add to its usefulness.

7.6 Future research possibilities

While this study has demonstrated that the small-firm setting provides a basis for complementary descriptive and analytical research on management accounting practice, it has also provided experience from which important research lessons can be drawn. Thus, the range of future research possibilities suggested is as follows:

- In this study the sample size was 82, and for many of the statistical tests the non-availability of data for some firms curtailed the number and range of firms which could be used. Future studies could benefit from a broader initial base of small firms.
- Given the variation found in management accounting practice, it would be of interest to base some future research on small-firm samples stratified by sector. This would permit investigation of whether or not type of business (e.g. service v. manufacturing) was a basis for different accounting practice.

- By definition, this study only included small firms which remained in existence. Some further interesting insights into management accounting would be obtained from a study which included, or indeed focused on, small firms which had failed.
- This study gathered data primarily from periodic interviews with owner-managers. Alternative sources and means of data gathering would enhance future research. For example:
  (a) the inclusion of other lower-level staff and those with responsibility for the production of internal accounting information;
  (b) the direct observation of accounting information creation and use in business operations;
  (c) the specific study of important developments such as the recruitment of management accounting staff for the first time or the introduction of new types of management accounting information.

While the primary focus of this study was on fundamental drivers of management accounting development, its findings provide a foundation for more applied research. For example, the specific uses of management accounting at different levels in the firm, stated information needs of managers and the capacity of management accounting to meet these needs, in terms of speed and information content in difficult settings, are all areas where valuable practical insights can be obtained. From future work of this type, the small firm provides an opportunity to allow researchers to explore and explain the circumstances which give rise to the birth of management accounting systems and their early formative development. It thus provides a basis for fundamental research into the nature and rationale of management accounting practice.

Appendix: Administered Questionnaire

Development of MAS

1 *Who prepares accounting information within your firm?*
[Tick all that apply and enter years in digits]

Staff involved	Qualification (articled/trainee, school, college/university, professional)				Years of accounting experience	
	Art.	*Schl.*	*Col.*	*Prof.*	*Within this firm*	*Since completing training*
(a) ☐ Owner						
(b) ☐ Accountant						
(c) ☐ Manager						
(d) ☐ Partner						
(e) ☐ Director						
(f) ☐ Executive						
(g) ☐ Clerk						
(h) ☐ Supervisor						
(i) ☐ Secretary						
(j) ☐ Assistant						
(k) ☐ Another						

1.1 What proportion of their time does the principal preparer of accounting information allocate to this task within a week?

_______________________________ %

2 *Which of the following types of information are available within your firm?*

	Set as budget/target?		Recorded as actual amount?		Frequency of measurement? (e.g. every 2/3/6 months)	Importance in managing the firm? (1=low, 5=high)				
	Yes	*No*	*Yes*	*No*		*1*	*2*	*3*	*4*	*5*
(a) Profit and loss										
(b) Balance sheet										
(c) Cash flow										
(d) Bank balance										

3 *Could you tell me if you use any of the following methods to decide about capital investment? When did you first use them (month/year)?*

	Used?	When?
(a) Return on investment, i.e. a measure of profit ÷ a measure of investment	☐	________
(b) Residual income, i.e. net surplus on a project	☐	________
(c) Net present value, i.e. net discounted project cash flow	☐	________
(d) Internal rate of return project	☐	________
(e) Payback period, i.e. years to positive net cash flow	☐	________

4 *I shall describe some methods for managing costs. For those methods that you use, could you tell me when they were first implemented (m/y)?*

	Used?	When?
(a) Modern production practices e.g. JIT, automated manufacturing	☐	________
(b) Modern accounting practices e.g. ABC, throughput accounting	☐	________
(c) Quantitative risk analysis e.g. expected outcomes, decision trees	☐	________
(d Value analysis e.g. by identifying products or activities that do not add value	☐	________
(e) Strategic pricing e.g. product life-cycle pricing, price discrimination	☐	________
(f) Transfer pricing e.g. using profit centres, pricing of components	☐	________

5 *The next question is concerned with how information flows around your business.*

5.1 Do you think about your business as being split up into groups or divisions, or simply as being just a single unit?

(a) Groups/Divisions/Branches ☐ (b) Single unit ☐

If (a), when (m/y) did you first start viewing your business in this way? ________

5.2 For the various types of information available within your business (e.g. sales, profit, cash flow, work effort, bank balance), do you ever segment them on any of the following bases?

(a) ☐ Product or product group
(b) ☐ Department or division of workgroup
(c) ☐ Geographical area
(d) ☐ Customer
(e) ☐ Any other (please specify)

5.3 Do you use spreadsheets or other computer software for handling information within your business?

(a) Yes ☐ (b) No ☐

If 'Yes', for which of the following do you use this technique, and when (m/y) did you first start doing so?

	Used?	When first used?
(a) Storing data	☐	________
(b) Project appraisal, e.g. NPV, IRR	☐	________
(c) Financial modelling	☐	________
(d) Forecasting and simulation	☐	________
(e) Sensitivity analysis	☐	________

6 6.1 Do management get regular accounting information which:

(a) ☐ measures performance?
(b) ☐ contains budget targets?
(c) ☐ shows the financial implications of specific decisions?
(d) ☐ other **[please specify]** ________

Not applicable ☐ **Go to Q.7**

6.2 Has this information developed over time?

(a) Yes ☐ (b) No ☐ **Go to Q.7**

6.3 In what important ways has it changed?

____

____

____

____

7 *Would you say any of the following factors have influenced the introduction/development of accounting information?*

(a) ☐ Growth in sales?
(b) ☐ Growth in number of employees?
(c) ☐ Growth in product lines?
(d) ☐ Change in organisational structure?
(e) ☐ Experiencing problems in performance?
(f) ☐ Increasing complexity in the operational process?
(g) ☐ The introduction of new capital (equity or loan)?

8 *I am interested in the complexity of your use of accounting information, so could I ask you whether you use such accounting information for:*
[Please tick all that apply, otherwise leave blank]

8.1 *Effective Planning and Analysis?* Do you do this to:

(a) ☐ keep within budget
(b) ☐ identify cost-cutting opportunities
(c) ☐ identify productivity-raising opportunities
(d) ☐ identify possibilities for improving product design
(e) ☐ identify growth opportunities
(f) ☐ reach specified levels of profit
(g) ☐ motivate employees by setting targets
(h) ☐ analyse business performance against projected or target values
(i) ☐ justify proposed expenditures
(j) ☐ measure performance of individual employees
(k) ☐ measure performance of teams of employees

8.2 *Activation and Direction of Daily Operations?* Do you do this to:

(a) ☐ identify trends
(b) ☐ assess and manage stock levels
(c) ☐ evaluate product performance
(d) ☐ calculate effects of marginal changes in costs and revenue
(e) ☐ identify standards within the firm which need revision
(f) ☐ identify operations which have become inefficient
(g) ☐ ensure products conform to quality standards
(h) ☐ measure customer service/satisfaction
(i) ☐ measure use of work time
(j) ☐ measure speed of production

8.3 *Problem-solving and Decision-making?* Do you do this to:

(a) ☐ evaluate or choose between alternative actions
(b) ☐ assess a new project or investment
(c) ☐ fix prices
(d) ☐ determine output levels
(e) ☐ determine schedule of production
(f) ☐ determine balance between in-house production and subcontracting
(g) ☐ analyse riskiness of a new idea
(h) ☐ decide whether or not to shut down whole or part of the business
(i) ☐ decide whether to sell off assets or part of the business
(j) ☐ decide whether to replace old assets with new assets
(k) ☐ determine number of products
(l) ☐ determine remuneration of staff
(m) ☐ assess staff for promotion/demotion

9 9.1 Do you consider accounting information produced for you to be reliable?

(a) Yes ☐ (b) No ☐ (c) Not applicable ☐

9.2 Why? ______________________________

10 10.1 Do you have difficulty in using accounting information?

(a) Yes ☐ (b) No ☐ (c) Not applicable ☐

10.2 Why? ______________________________

References

Acs, Z. and Audretsch, D. (1988) 'Innovations in large and small firms: an empirical analysis', *American Economic Review* 78(4), 678–90.

Acs, Z., Carlsson, B. and Karlsson, C. (eds) (1999) *Entrepreneurship, Small and Medium-sized Enterprises and the Macroeconomy*. Cambridge University Press; Cambridge.

Anderson, S.W. (1995) 'A framework of assessing cost management changes: the case of activity based costing implementation at General Motors 1986–1993', *Journal of Management Accounting Research,* Fall.

Baiman, S. (1982) 'Agency research in managerial accounting: a survey', *Journal of Accounting Literature* 1, 154–209.

Birch, D. (1996) Open discussion on SMEs and Job Creation. Global workshop on Entrepreneurship. Jönköping International Business School, Sweden.

Brehmer, B. (1990) 'Strategies in real-time, dynamic decision making'. In R.M. Hogarth (ed.), *Insights in Decision Making: A Tribute to Hillel J. Einhorn.* Chicago University Press; Chicago (pp. 262–79).

Burns, T. and Stalker, G. (1961) *The Management of Innovation,* Tavistock Institute; London.

Burns, W.J. and Waterhouse, J.H. (1975) 'Budgetary control and organisational structure', *Journal of Accounting Research* 13, 177–203.

Carsberg, B.V., Page, M.J., Sindal, A.J. and Waring, I.D. (1985) *Small Company Financial Reporting.* Prentice-Hall International; London.

Casson, M. (1994) 'Economic perspectives on business information'. In L. Bud-Frierman (ed.), *Information Acumen: The understanding and use of knowledge in modern business.* Routledge; London (ch. 7).

Chandler, A.D. (1962) *Strategy and Structure.* MIT Press; Cambridge, Mass.

Chang, C-H. and Jevons Lee, C-W. (1992) 'Information acquisition as business strategy', *Southern Economic Journal* 58(3), 750–61.

Chapman, C.S. (1997) 'Reflections on a contingent view of accounting', *Accounting, Organizations and Society* 22, 189–206.

Coase, R. (1937) 'The nature of the firm', *Economica* 4, 386–405.

Coase, R.H. (1990) 'Accounting and the theory of the firm', *Journal of Accounting and Economics* 12, 3–13.

Cooper, R. (1989) 'The rise of activity-based costing – Part Four: What do activity based cost systems look like?' *Journal of Cost Management,* Spring, 38–49.

Daly, M.A. and McCann, A. (1992) 'How many small firms?', *Employment Gazette* 100(2), 47–51.

Davidson, R., Lindmark, L. and Olofsson, C. (1999) 'Job creation during a recession and recovery', Ch. 10 in Acs, Carlsson and Karlsson (eds) pp. 286–309.

Department for Education and Employment (1996) 'Small firms' training needs, practices and difficulties', *Labour Market Quarterly Report,* November.

Eliasson, G. (1996) *Firm Objectives, Control and Organization: The Use of Information and the Transfer of Knowledge within the Firm.* Kluwer; Dordrecht.

Emmanuel, C. and Otley, D. (1986) *Accounting for Management Control.* Van Nostrand Reinhold; Wokingham.

Ezzamel, M. and Hart, H. (1987) *Advanced Management Accounting, An Organisation Emphasis.* Cassell; London.

Fang, B. (1990) 'The user survey and design conception of information systems for the county of Chong Ming (Shanghai)'. In K. Ganzhorn and S. Faustoferri (eds), *Bridging the Information Gap for Small and Medium Enterprises.* Springer-Verlag; Berlin (pp. 219–27).

Flamholtz, D.T. (1983) 'The markets and hierarchies framework: a critique of the model's applicability to accounting and economic development', *Accounting, Organizations and Society* 8, 147–51.

Gall, H. (1990) 'Technology broker systems for SMEs in FRG'. In K. Ganzhorn and F. Faustoferri (eds), *Bridging the Information Gap for Small and Medium Enterprises.* Springer-Verlag; Berlin (pp. 151–60).

Ganzhorn, K. and Faustoferri, S. (eds) (1990) *Bridging the Information Gap for Small and Medium Enterprises.* Springer-Verlag; Berlin.

Garnsey, E. (1998) 'A study of the early growth of the firm', *Industrial and Corporate Change* 7(3), 523–56.

Gordon, L.A. and Miller, D. (1976). 'A contingency framework for the design of accounting information systems', *Accounting, Organizations and Society* 1, 59–70.

Gul, F.A. (1991) 'The effects of management accounting systems and environmental uncertainty on small business managers' performance', *Accounting and Business Research* 22(85), 57–61.

Hayes, D. (1977) 'The contingency theory of management accounting', *The Accounting Review* 52.

Hicks, D. T. (1992) *Activity Based Costing for Small and Medium Sized Businesses.* Wiley; London.

Hollins, R. (1983) *Simplecost – The Small Printer's Guide to Costing.* Comprint Services; Sutton Coldfield.

Holmes, S., Kelly, G. and Cunningham, R. (1991) 'The small firm information cycle: a reappraisal', *International Small Business Journal* 4, 41–53.

Holmes, S. and Nicholls, D. (1989) 'Modelling the accounting information requirements of small businesses', *Accounting and Business Research* 19(74), 143–50.

IFAC/CIMA (1998) *Financial Management Fundamentals.* London.

Jarvis, R., Kitching, J., Curran, J. and Lightfoot, G. (1996) *The Financial Management of Small Firms: An Alternative Perspective.* Certified Accountants Educational Trust; London.

Jensen, M.C. and Meckling, W.H. (1976) 'Theory of the firm: managerial behaviour, agency costs and ownership structure', *Journal of Financial Economics,* October, 305–60.

Johnson, H.T. (1983) 'The search for gain in markets and firms: a review of the historical emergence of management accounting systems', *Accounting, Organizations and Society* 8, 139–46.

Jones, C.S. (1985) 'An empirical study of the evidence for contingency theories of management accounting systems in conditions of rapid change', *Accounting, Organizations and Society* 10, 303–28.

Jordan, J.S. (1989) 'The economics of accounting information systems', *American Economic Review* 79(2), 140–5.

Jordan, J.S. (1999) 'Management accounting in activity networks', CRIEFF Discussion Paper No. 9912, Department of Economics, University of St Andrews.

Jorrisen, A., Laveren, E. and Devinck, S. (1997a) Planning and Control: Necessary Tools for Success in Small and Medium-sized Enterprises? Empirical Results of Survey and Core Research on SMEs in Belgium. Paper presented to the 20th Annual Congress of the European Accounting Association, Graz.

Jorrisen, A., Laveren, E., Devinck, S. and Vanstraelen, A. (1997b) Planning and Control: Are they Necessary Tools for Success? Empirical Results of Survey and Core Research on Small and Medium-sized Enterprises compared with Empirical Research on Large Enterprises. Paper presented to the 8th World Congress of the International Association for Accounting Education and Research, Paris.

Kao, J.L. and Hughes, J.S. (1993) 'Note on risk aversion and sharing of firm specific information in duopolies', *Journal of Industrial Economics* 41, 103–12.

Kaplan, R.S. (1982) *Advanced Management Accounting.* Prentice-Hall; Englewood Cliffs, NJ.

Kaplan, R.S. (1994) 'Management accounting (1984–1994): development of new practice and theory', *Management Accounting Research* 3/4.

Keynes, J.M. (1921) *A Treatise on Probability.* Macmillan; London.

Knight, F.H. (1921) *Risk, Uncertainty and Profit.* Chicago University Press (Stigler edn 1971); Chicago.

Langfield-Smith, K. (1997) 'Management control systems and strategy: a critical review', *Accounting, Organizations and Society* 22, 207–32.

Lawrence, P.R. and Lorch, J.W. (1967) Organisation and Environment: Managing Differentiation and Integration. Graduate School of Business Administration, Harvard University.

Levy, M. and Powell, P. (1998), 'SME flexibility and the role of the information system', *Small Business Economics* 11(2), 183–96.

Libby, T. and Waterhouse, J.H. (1996) 'Predicting change in management accounting systems', *Journal of Management Accounting Research* 8, 137–50.

Lybaert, N. (1998) 'The information use in an SME: its importance and some elements of influence', *Small Business Economics* 10(2), 171–91.

Miles, M.B. and Huberman, A.M. (1984) *Qualitative Data Analysis: A Sourcebook of New Methods.* London: Sage.

Mitchell, F., Reid, G.C. and Smith, J.A. (1998) 'A case for researching management accounting in SMEs', *Management Accounting,* October 1998, 30–2.

Mitchell, F., Reid, G.C. and Terry, N.G. (1995) 'Post investment demand for accounting information by venture capitalists', *Accounting and Business Research,* 25(99), 186–96.

Mitchell, F., Reid, G.C. and Terry, N.G. (1997) 'Venture capital supply and accounting information system development', *Entrepreneurship Theory and Practice,* Summer, 45–62.

Mitchell, F., Reid, G.C. and Smith, J. (1998) 'A case for researching management accounting in SMEs', *Management Accounting,* October, 30–32.

Monden, Y. and Hamada, K. (1991) 'Target costing and Kaisen costing in Japanese automobile companies', *Journal of Management Accounting Research,* Fall.

Nayak, A. and Greenfield, S. (1994). 'The use of management accounting information for managing micro business'. In A. Hughes and D. Storey (eds), *Finance and the Small Firm.* Routledge; London.

Otley, D. (1980) 'The contingency theory of management accounting: achievement and prognosis', *Accounting, Organizations and Society* 5, 413–428.

Pavitt, K., Robson, M. and Townsend, J. (1987) 'The size distribution of innovating firms in the UK – 1945–1983', *Journal of Industrial Economics* 15(3), 297–316.

Perry, C.A. (1963) *Management Accounting for the Small Business.* The Association of Certified Accountants; London.

Perry, C.A. (1968) *Management Accounting for the Small Business* (5th imp.). The Association of Certified Accountants; London.

Porter, M.E. (1980) *Competitive Strategy: Techniques for Analyzing Industries and Competitors.* Free Press; New York.

Quah, D.T. (1997) 'Increasingly weightless economies', *Bank of England Quarterly Bulletin* 37(1), 49–56.

Radner, R. (1985) 'The internal economy of large firms', *Economic Journal* 81, 547–62.

Raymond, L. and Magnenat-Thalmann, N. (1982) 'Information systems in small business: are they used in managerial decisions?', *American Journal of Small Business* 6(4), 20–6.

Reid, G.C. (1987a) *Theories of Industrial Organisation.* Basil Blackwell; Oxford.

Reid, G.C. (1987b) 'Applying field research techniques to the business enterprise', *International Journal of Social Economics* 14(11), 3–25.

Reid, G.C. (1993) *Small Business Enterprise – An Economic Analysis.* Routledge; London.

Reid, G.C. (1996) 'Mature micro-firms and their experience of funding shortages', *Small Business Economics* 8, 27–37.

Reid, G.C. (1998) *Venture Capital Investment: An Agency Analysis of Practice.* Routledge; London.

Reid, G.C. (1999) 'Capital structure at inception and the short-run performance of micro-firms', Ch. 7 in Acs, Carlsson and Karlsson (eds) pp. 186–205.

Reid, G.C. and Roberts, C.J. (1996) 'Performance implications of patent family size'. In A. Belcher, J. Hassard and S. Procter (eds), *R&D Decisions: Strategy, Policy and Innovations.* Routledge; London.

Reid, G.C., Smith, J.A. and Siler, P.A. (1996) 'The quality of patenting in the UK scientific instruments industry'. In A. Webster and K. Packer (eds), *Innovation and the Intellectual Property System.* Kluwer Law International; Dordrecht, pp. 23–46.

Reid, G.C., Terry, N.G. and Smith, J.A. (1997) 'Risk management in venture capital investor–investee relations', *European Journal of Finance* 3(1), 27–47.

Romano, C.A. and Ratnatunga, J. (1994) 'Growth stages of small manufacturing firms: the relationship with planning and control', *Public Policy* 13(1), 173–95.

Scapens, R.W. (1991) *Management Accounting, A Review of Recent Developments.* Macmillan; Basingstoke.

Scottish Enterprise (1996) *Scottish New Business Statistics: Annual 1996,* with The Committee of Scottish Clearing Banks; Glasgow.

Sekaran, U. (1992) *Research Methods for Business: A Skill Building Approach.* John Wiley; New York.

Simon, H.A. (1972) 'Theories of bounded rationality'. In C. McGuire and R. Radner (eds) *Decision and Organization.* North-Holland; Amsterdam (pp. 161–76).

Slovic, P., Griffin, D. and Tversky, A. (1990) 'Compatibility effects in judgement and choice'. In R.M. Hogarth (ed.), *Insights in Decision Making: A Tribute to Hillel J. Einhorn.* Chicago University Press; Chicago (pp. 5–27).

Snow, A.B. (1967) *The Preparation of Interim Accounts for Management in the Smaller Manufacturing Concern.* The General Educational Trust of the Institute of Chartered Accountants in England and Wales; London.

Storey, D.J. (1994) *Understanding the Small Business Sector.* Thomson Business Press; London.

Tiessen, P. and Waterhouse, J.H. (1983) 'Towards a descriptive theory of management accounting', *Accounting, Organizations and Society* 8.

Trindade, S.C. (1990) *Preface.* In K. Ganzhorn and S. Faustoferri (eds), *Bridging the Information Gap for Small and Medium Enterprises.* Springer-Verlag; Berlin (pp. v–vi).

Wallsten, T.S. (1990) 'The costs and benefits of vague information'. In R.M. Hogarth (ed.), *Insights in Decision Making: A Tribute to Hillel J. Einhorn.* Chicago University Press; Chicago (pp. 28–43).

Waterhouse, J.H. and Tiessen, P. (1978) 'A contingency framework for management accounting research', *Accounting, Organizations and Society* 3, 65–76.

Williamson, O.E. (1970) *Corporate Control and Business Behaviour.* Prentice-Hall; Englewood Cliffs, NJ.

Williamson, O.E. (1972) 'Markets hierarchies and modern corporation', *Journal of Economic Behaviour and Organisation* 17.

Williamson, O.E. (1975) *Markets and Hierarchies: Analysis and Antitrust Implications.* Free Press; New York.

Williamson, O.E. (1992) 'Markets, hierarchies and the modern corporation – an unfolding perspective', *Journal of Economic Behaviour and Organization* 17(3), 335–52.

Woodward, J. (1958) *Management and Technology.* HMSO; London.

Woodward, J. (1965) *Industrial Organisation: Theory and Practice.* Oxford University Press.

Wynarczyk, P.R., Watson, D.J., Storey, H., Short, H. and Keasey, K. (1993) *The Managerial Labour Market in Small and Medium-sized Enterprises.* Routledge; London.

Yin, Robert K. (1993) *Applications of Case Study Research.* Sage Publications; London.

Zhiyou, Z. (1990) 'Information needs of small and medium enterprises'. In K. Ganzhorn and S. Faustoferri (eds), *Bridging the Information Gap for Small and Medium Enterprises.* Springer-Verlag, Berlin (pp. 23–34).

Zimmerman, J.L. (1979) 'The costs and benefits of cost allocations', *The Accounting Review,* July, 504–21.